The Place That Inhabits Us

Poems of the San Francisco Bay Watershed

The Place That Inhabits Us

Poems of the San Francisco Bay Watershed

Selected by Sixteen Rivers Press

SIXTEEN RIVERS PRESS

Published by Sixteen Rivers Press

P. O. Box 640663

San Francisco, CA 94164-0663

www.sixteenrivers.org

Library of Congress Control Number: 2009942894

ISBN: 978-0-9819816-1-1

Front-cover art: *The Golden Gate from Grizzly Peak*, copyright © Tom Killion, 2008. See complete image at tomkillion.com.

The members of Sixteen Rivers Press would like to thank everyone who helped with the creation of this book, especially those who allowed us to use their poems and those who brought other people's work to our attention.

We would like to thank the National Endowment for the Arts for its past support.

We extend our deep gratitude to Tom Killion for the generous use of his artwork for the cover.

And for responding to our request for a foreword with such vitality, we thank Robert Hass, whose own work as poet, essayist, and activist has done so much to shape our understanding of watersheds, natural and literary.

Finally, we would like to thank the subscribers and supporters of Sixteen Rivers Press; without them, this book, and the press itself, would not exist.

Contents

Foreword by Robert Hass   ix

Introduction   xv

This Air

August Kleinzahler, *Land's End*   3

Adrienne Rich, from *An Atlas of the Difficult World*   5

Tung-hui Hu, *Balance*   6

Gary Soto, *Waterwheel*   7

Camille Dungy, *Where bushes periodically burn, children fear other children: girls*   8

Robin Leslie Jacobson, *Wildfire Season*   9

Peter Everwine, *Back from the Fields*   10

Jane Mead, *The Laden Henceforth Pending*   11

David St. John, *Peach Fires*   12

Josephine Miles, *Apart from Branches*   13

Forrest Hamer, *Origins*   14

Phyllis Koestenbaum, *Landmarks*   15

Mark Doty, *Esta Noche*   16

Ursula Le Guin, *April in San José*   18

Quinton Duval, *One Bright Morning*   19

Morton Marcus, *The Poem for Gonzales, California*   20

B. A. Bishop, *Wally Watch*   22

Stella Beratlis, *Patterson Pass*   23

Charlotte Muse, *Rattlesnake*   24

Patrick Daly, *Bronze Horse Cast from Driftwood—Do Not Touch*   25

John Isles, *Lighthouse*   26

Shuddering Back to This Coastline

Zbigniew Herbert, *Sequoia*   29

Jack Marshall, *Her Flag*   30

Stefanie Marlis, *Golden Hat*   31

D. A. Powell, *california poppy*   32

Mark Turpin, *The Aftermath*   33

Jean V. Gier, *California Coast*   35

Daniel Tobin, *A Cone of the Eucalyptus*   36

Alejandro Murguía, *16th & Valencia*   37

Tom McCarthy, *He walked through the roughest part of town . . .*   38

Martín Espada, *Two Mexicanos Lynched in Santa Cruz, California, May 3, 1877*   39

Thom Gunn, *The J Car*   40

Linda Gregg, *Death Looks Down*   42

Constance Crawford, *Confluence*   43

Chana Bloch, *Blue-Black*   44

Jeanne Lohmann, *A Place to Live*   45

Ellen Dudley, *A Blessing*   46

Gary Young, *The Signature Mark of Autumn*   47

Gillian Conoley, *Next and the Corner*   48

Like One Eternity Touching Another

Gary Snyder, *Home from the Sierra*   51

Aaron Shurin, from *Involuntary Lyrics*   52

Walt Whitman, *Facing West from California's Shores*   53

Lee Herrick, *Ars Poetica*   54

Yehuda Amichai, *North of San Francisco*   55

Brenda Hillman, *Practical Water*   56

Lew Welch, *The Song Mt. Tamalpais Sings*   59

Marilyn Chin, *Art Wong Is Alive and Ill and Struggling in Oakland, California*   60

Daniel Polikoff, *Seen from the Miwok Trail*   62

Nancy Cherry, *Hiking Through What Remains of the Mt. Vision Fire* 63

Czeslaw Milosz, *Gift* 64

Robert Hass, *For Czesław Miłosz in Kraków* 65

Priscilla Lee, *Burnt Offerings: Mother's Day at the Lees, 1999* 67

Al Young, *For Kenneth and Miriam Patchen* 68

Eliot Schain, *Bodhisattva West* 69

Donna Emerson, *The Wild Merced* 70

Sharon Fain, *Feather River* 71

Kathleen Winter, *Limbs* 72

Dan Clurman, *In a Doorway on Powell Street* 73

Ellery Akers, *The Word That Is a Prayer* 74

William Dickey, *The Rainbow Grocery* 75

Don Emblen, *As to Immortality* 76

Their Green Flanks

Kay Ryan, *Green Hills* 79

Robert Duncan, *Often I Am Permitted to Return to a Meadow* 80

C. Dale Young, *The Philosopher in Golden Gate Park* 81

Dana Gioia, *California Hills in August* 82

Jeff Knorr, *Foul Ball* 83

Thomas Centolella, *The Orders* 84

George Oppen, *Psalm* 86

Ellen Bass, *Birdsong from My Patio* 87

Barbara Swift Brauer, *Changing Forecast* 88

Joyce Jenkins, *Piano Man* 89

Karen Llagas, *Archipelago Dust* 90

Catharine Clark-Sayles, *Wild Fennel* 91

W. S. Di Piero, *The Little Flowers* 92

Sharon Doubiago, *Sequoia* 93

Julia Levine, *Golden Gate* 95

Molly Fisk, *Hunter's Moon*   96

Melody Lacina, *Rain in January*   97

Ann Fisher-Wirth, *At McClure's Beach, Point Reyes National Seashore, California*   98

Stephanie Mendel, *The Trip to Napa*   100

Sandra Gilbert, *November 26, 1992: Thanksgiving at the Sea Ranch . . .*   101

Between Fog and Drizzle

Diana O'Hehir, *Living on the Earthquake Fault*   105

Jane Hirshfield, *Dog and Bear*   106

Susan Kolodny, *Koi Pond, Oakland Museum*   107

Zara Raab, *Landscape with Snakes*   108

Jim Powell, *WL 8338*   109

Larry Levis, *The Poet at Seventeen*   110

Jim Nawrocki, *From Cole Street*   112

Kim Addonizio, *At Moss Beach*   113

Amber Flora Thomas, *Oak Leaf*   114

John Savant, *Bocce Ball: North Beach*   115

Robert Bly, *Welcoming a Child in the Limantour Dunes*   117

William Keener, *Bolinas Lagoon*   118

Ken Haas, *Land's End*   119

Carolyn Kizer, *The Great Blue Heron*   120

Laura Chester, *Last Breath*   122

Richard Silberg, *Sunset*   123

Alice Jones, *The Bay*   124

Joanne Kyger, *The Sun Is About to Pass*   125

Kenneth Rexroth, *Time Spirals*   126

Contributors' Notes   129

Permissions   137

Author Index   141

Foreword

The first anthology of a regional poetry was probably the set of words that the first members of the human species said to each other to signify the first things they felt the need to have sounds for. It is interesting to guess what those things were: the names of animals, of actions during hunting, of parts of the body, of kinship relations, of places on the earth and things in the air. It is a question whether song preceded or came after speech. If song came first, then it was possible for humans to convey anger and sadness and happiness and possibly wit even before there were words to utter. It would also be interesting to know whether laughter or speech came first. In any case, out of laughter, song, speech, dance probably, and perhaps some sense of the magical property of speech connected both to the power of naming and the speed speech gave to the evolution of memory, the first vocabulary— which was also, because it was remembered, the first anthology—came into being to create a fundamental relationship between people and the places where they live. This event seems to have occurred between 200,000 and 100,000 years ago.

There are rocks all over Northern California much older than that, and hundreds of plant and animal species. Speech, poetry, and anthologies of poetry are all quite young things on the earth. In Northern California this is especially so, because human beings seem not to have arrived here until some time between fifteen and twelve thousand years ago, just during and after the last ice age.

Perhaps because I grew up in and around San Francisco hearing stories about the great earthquake and fire of 1906, I tend to think of the history of California, like that wave of hunter-gatherers from Asia, as fires: sudden wild rushes of transforming energy sweeping across the land. The first fires were the ones that lifted the Sierra Nevada and the Coast Range hills into the air so that they formed the great Central Valley and the rivers that created San Francisco Bay and gave the region the contours that humans found here when they arrived. They were the second fire: they and their technologies and their speech. The first thing they seem to have done is hunt to extinction the megafauna that brought them here, as they tracked herds across the Aleutian land bridge. The second thing that they must have done in the process is make trails. Probably they followed animal paths that followed the paths made by water along rivers and streams as they drained into lakes and wetlands and coastal beaches. That must have been the order: first the movement of water and then the movement of animals and then the movement of humans along the animal paths, and a geography would have emerged, the kind of physical and mental map that, for humans, makes a place a place.

And these humans had already had speech for at least ten millennia. They arrived here just about the time when written languages were beginning to appear in Sumer and Egypt. And they came—in what must have been the successive waves of immigrants who peopled the Americas—speaking many languages, languages as distinct from one another as Hungarian and Chinese. For reasons that are still unclear, more different peoples speaking distinctly different languages settled in California than in all the rest of continental North America combined. Of the almost three hundred languages described by Europeans as they advanced across the continent, nearly eighty were spoken in the watersheds of Northern California. Some of the languages still survive. Most of them are extinct and survive in the vocabularies transcribed by Europeans, the first poignant anthologies of California's poetry of place: the words for *elbow* and *aunt* and *brown towhee* in the languages of people who have disappeared from the earth. And they survive in place names, which were the first human mapping of the landscape. The names—Yolo, Tamalpais, Tahoe, Napa—are Spanish and English hearings and mishearings of other people's languages, and they are also a kind of anthology and a remnant geography.

The next fire was the coming of the Spanish from Mexico. They arrived with the language that gave California its present name, which they took from a book of imaginary places. They arrived in this imaginary place in stages, and the feed they brought for their horses and livestock, and the burrs, awns, and seed heads of Mediterranean grasses caught in the manes and fetlocks of these creatures, were the principal physical form taken by this wave of fire. Within a generation, Mediterranean grasses swept through the Coast Range mountains and valleys and replaced almost completely the native bunchgrasses. The Spanish—who became Mexicans in 1821—settled the land thinly, and their ascendancy was brief. The region's next anthology consists of words they left on the land, place names like Santa Barbara, Paso Robles, and Contra Costa, and terms like *chaparral* and *sierra*, *arroyo* and *mesa*.

The next fire was the Gold Rush: the wildfire immigration of gold hunters, the seizing of California from Mexico, the clear-cutting of forests to feed the steam engines that got the forty-niners to the mines, the devastation of hydraulic mining, the English-language names that came with the prospectors and their culture, and the sensibility of pioneer naming: Emigrant Gap, Rough and Ready, Gold Run, Lime Kiln Flat. The poetry of this boom was probably the popular song—"My Darling

Clementine" and "Sweet Betsy from Pike"—and English-language California's first literary community began to form in San Francisco around a new magazine, *Overland Monthly,* consisting of Bret Harte, Ina Coolbrith, Charles Warren Stoddard, the acerbic Ambrose Bierce, and the first native-born poet, Edwin Markham, who grew up in the Sacramento Valley. It was a beginning, but the one writer to emerge in this period who gave fundamental shape to the way the people of the region saw their place and themselves was John Muir, most of all in the publication of his *Mountains of California* in 1894.

The next fire was *the* fire: the earthquake of 1906 and the hastily thrown-up nineteenth-century city that it burned down. These twinned events brought the twentieth century to San Francisco Bay and the countryside of the Shasta watershed. In its way, the first decades of the new century brought changes as dramatic as those wrought by the first Asian immigrants from the Aleutian land bridge with their hunting technologies, or the Spanish with their armies and missions and cattle, or the Yankees and their trains and their telegraph. Between 1900 and 1950, the population of the Bay Area grew from 660,000 to 2,680,000 people.

This required water, for domestic and industrial use and for irrigated land to feed the population. San Francisco turned for water to the Yosemite region's Hetch Hetchy River and its dramatic glacially carved valley, which the city proposed to dam. Muir bitterly resisted this proposal—the Yosemite had just been made a national park and its wild lands placed off limits for development—and he was defeated. Shaughnessy Dam began construction in 1910. In California, the saying went, all politics become water politics. In 1919, the U.S. Geological Survey developed a plan to deliver Sacramento River water to the farmlands of the Central Valley. In 1927, the East Bay built a pipeline to supply itself with Mokelumne River water. This was a period of epic hydrological engineering. Hoover Dam went up in 1931 and 1932. And it was during this period that California became one of the most engineered landscapes on earth, as it figured out how to make the water from the Sierra and the rainy north flow south to supply a burgeoning agriculture and an exploding Los Angeles. The Central Valley Plan (the engineering that would make it happen) was on the boards in 1933. Construction began in 1937. By 1940, California was delivering the Colorado River to Central Valley farms and to golf courses in the desert.

During these years, the region began to produce something of a literary culture. A. L. Kroeber, a Berkeley anthropologist, produced a *Handbook of the Indians of California* (1925), which translated at least some of the language of the land's first inhabitants. The young Jack London began to make fiction of this place, including *Martin Eden* (1910). In 1924, in Carmel, Robinson Jeffers, the Scots-Irish son of a Calvinist theologian, published *Tamar, Roan Stallion, and Other Poems.* Yvor

Winters arrived at Stanford in 1928, and Josephine Miles at Berkeley in 1932. Kenneth Rexroth came to San Francisco in 1928 as a self-invented radical, painter, and cubist poet; his first book, *In What Hour* (1941), was the next decisive event in the culture of poetry that gave the place a way to see itself.

So the region, hardly a hundred years old in the English language, was beginning to have a language and a culture of its own when the next fire, World War II, swept through it. Hundreds of thousands of Americans passed through San Francisco on their way to the Pacific war, and many of them liked what they saw and returned to stay. Between 1950 and 2000, growing in population from 2,680,000 to 6,740,000, the Bay Area became one sprawling conurbation, from the suburbs in the foothills of the Sierra north of Sacramento, through Oakland and San Francisco to San Jose and the suburbs of Carmel Valley. The Central Valley became during these years the most potent agricultural economy in the world. Downtown San Francisco became a forest of tall commercial buildings. Shipbuilding and other war industries had drawn large numbers of African American workers from Texas and the Deep South, and Oakland in the postwar years became a predominantly African American city. Electronic technologies created the Silicon Valley, with San Jose as its center. The truck farms and small dairies became suburbs, and the margins of the bay were being eaten by development. The racist immigration laws of the first decade of the century were repealed, and Asian immigration—mostly from China and Taiwan, Korea and Vietnam and India—resumed the region's rich mix of Pacific cultures.

One of the servicemen who passed through was a naval officer named Lawrence Ferlinghetti—and one might mark the beginning of this next era in the history of poetry in the region from his founding of City Lights, the country's first all-paperback bookstore, a radical bit of entrepreneurship, in 1953. Though there are other dates to mark as well: the coming together of Robert Duncan, Jack Spicer, and Robin Blaser in undergraduate classes at Berkeley in 1945; the arrival of Gary Snyder and Philip Whalen in Berkeley in 1953, of the young English poet Thom Gunn at Stanford in 1954, and of Allen Ginsberg and Jack Kerouac in San Francisco in 1955; and Ruth Witt-Diamant's founding of the San Francisco State University Poetry Center in 1954.

Robert Duncan would say of this time, "We all came out of Papa Rexroth's overcoat." Since the late thirties, Rexroth had held Friday-night salons at his San Francisco home that gathered the writers, artists, and political activists of the city to talk about politics and art and to read poetry, and that made the cultural life of the city for two decades. And Rexroth was writing poems of the city, the Marin mountains and coast, and the Sierra Nevada that, following Jeffers (whom he detested), began to make a regional poetry that was not merely regional. He imagined a city, a region, and a poetry that was at once local and cosmopolitan, innovative, urban, alive to nature, politically aware, permeable to both Asia and Europe, impelled by philosophical and religious quests to make sense of experience in a violent time. He arrived a believing Anglican, and he migrated, partly through his work on Chinese and Japanese poetry, to Buddhism. He experimented in the clubs—West Coast jazz was emerging in those years—with the idea of a public art through the mix of new poetry and new music, and he did commentaries on literature for the region's (and the country's) first nonprofit radio station.

These decades were quite a run, but they are not the end of the story. Czeslaw Milosz would arrive at Berkeley in 1960 and begin to write some of the most extraordinary poems of the century from Grizzly Peak in the Berkeley hills. George Oppen came here to write his late poems of San Francisco. Ishmael Reed and Al Young met in Berkeley in 1967 and began to edit a magazine reflecting all the cultures of the region. Their arrival and the beginnings of a new California Latino writing—Luis Omar Salinas, *Crazy Gypsy* (1970); Gary Soto, *Elements of San Joaquin* (1976); Lorna Dee Cervantes, *Emplumada* (1981)—and of an Asian American poetry are also part of the story, as is the emergence in the 1980s of a third- or fourth-generation avant-garde in the form of Language poetry and poetics in San Francisco and Berkeley, and a new feminist experimental writing in San Francisco around Kathleen Fraser and her magazine HOW(*ever*). Since the 1970s, partly because of the remarkable vortex of poets and poems that the region produced in the 1950s and 1960s, Northern California has been lively with poets practicing their craft, drawing on the range of aesthetic and cultural traditions. A hundred and fifty years into the presence of the English language on the land—not very long by Greek or Chinese standards—there are many, many voices, a complicated root system, and a watershed still under stress and changing.

Probably that is a place to end this narrative and let the poems speak for themselves. It was the San Franciscan Robert Frost who said that the land was ours before we were the land's, and if we don't wreck it altogether, we will be a long time saying what it is like to live here. If you think of China or Greece, cultures that have had a shared and evolving written record of their experience of place for three thousand years, it will seem that what we have here is the barest beginning. One of the great pleasures of this anthology is that, at a certain moment, a group of early-twenty-first-century poets made a selection of poems about the place that mattered to them, so that this book is about the experience of place—and about being given the remembered expression of the experience of place by others who have lived here. And that begins to be a culture.

—*Robert Hass*
Berkeley, October 2009

Introduction

The Sea said "Come" to the Brook—
The Brook said "Let me grow"—
The Sea said "Then you will be a Sea—
I want a Brook—Come now"!
—EMILY DICKINSON

In 1999, seven poets came together to create a press based in the San Francisco Bay Area. The founders, living throughout the region, formed a shared-work, nonprofit collective, hoping to publish two books a year. They named the press Sixteen Rivers, for the web of major waterways that flow into San Francisco Bay, but also for the richness of metaphor the name suggested: poetry as a confluence of voices, language, feeling, tradition—an ecology of sorts—that, like a river, enriches the life of a place.

With the help of generous subscribers, donors, and the good faith of the poetry world, the press flourished. After publishing the books of its founders, in 2003 Sixteen Rivers Press opened its doors to blind submissions with the provision that selected poets become members of the collective for a three-year stint, helping to run the press: selecting and editing new books; supervising design, printing and distribution; and managing the finances.

Ten years have passed since the press was founded: ten years, twenty books (all still in print), one compact disc, a grant from the National Endowment for the Arts, local and national awards, and an ongoing series of public readings around the greater Bay Area, from Modesto to Sonoma, Palo Alto to Point Reyes Station, and now, to celebrate our first decade, this anthology: a gathering of poems of place, poems of our watershed.

Watershed: the gathering ground of rivers that nourish and drain a discrete region. But also, a sphere of culture, a gathering ground for art and ideas. The poems collected here, drawn from our own Mt. Shasta watershed, embody what it's like to live in—to *in*-habit—this place: the astonishing weave of cities and towns, landscape and language, climate and history that make up the greater San Francisco Bay Area. From the granite slopes of the Sierra to the Delta, through the Coastal Range to the bay and shores of the Pacific, here is a collection of poems that map this improbable place—poems that contain, in Wallace Stevens's wonderful phrase, "the intelligence of their soil."

We selected poems for the book in two ways: Half were chosen from a nationally publicized call that brought in over a thousand submissions, and half were chosen from a group of over two hundred poems nominated by members of the press. We asked for "poems of place set in the greater San Francisco Bay Area," interpreting *place* broadly as natural, cultural, or psychological space. We were looking for a mix of voices and styles, work that gave insight, life, and dimension to our theme. And we were looking for a mix of poets—well known, unknown, and in between. But most of all, we were looking for poems that shed light on the many facets of life in this region. Our one rule: No poems by authors published by Sixteen Rivers Press.

At first, we arranged the poems alphabetically by last names, from Ellery Akers to Gary Young, and were fascinated to see the sparks between poems that some of these adjacencies created. Some seemed downright revelatory, poems responding to each other across time and circumstance, the living and the dead, gathering energy, often through opposition. Thom Gunn, for example, climbing through San Francisco in "The J Car" to call on a dying friend, graphs strangely yet precisely onto Linda Gregg's "Death Looks Down," where salmon are tracked to the end of their run, the figure of Death "facing the constant motion." We wondered whether the whole book could be organized around this notion of a lively gathering of poems, speaking to one another, opening doors onto one another, sometimes taking issue, sometimes consoling and affirming. So we dropped the alphabetical order and began to listen to the conversation.

We saw Robert Duncan's solitary meadow of the mind shedding light on C. Dale Young's philosopher lying on the grass at Golden Gate Park; we heard Yehuda Amichai's Jerusalem-drenched meditation on the beach in Bolinas frame and energize Brenda Hillman's moral engagement with her neighborhood creek. Jack Marshall's loony moment of laughter, "schlepping a sack of compost soil," became all the more joyous when set beside the chilling eternity Zbigniew Herbert found in the stump of an ancient sequoia. Listening in this way, we sorted the poems into five sections, each a thread of call and response. Such discoveries became for us the great and unexpected pleasure of the book—like finding between two poems something new, another poem almost, an undiscovered niche in the terrain—"the place," in Stella Beratlis's haunting phrase, "that inhabits us."

We hope you'll follow the threads of these sections, listening for such moments: Adrienne Rich, walking the coast, describing the exilic feel of many a late arrival, saying, "This is no place you ever knew me," is immediately enjoined by Tung-Hui Hu's anxious story, "Soon after I moved to California. . . ." "This is the last place,"

Lew Welch has Mt. Tamalpais say, "nowhere else to go. . . . " No, not really, says Whitman, staring east from his imagined Pacific shore, chanting, "the circle almost circled . . . now I face home again. . . . "

As you turn the pages of this book, traveling the entire watershed, we hope you'll discover some sparks of your own: There are egrets and grievous losses here; prayers, panhandlers, Delta mornings and sunsets in the 'hood; the fog, certainly, and the bridges, but a spirit from Kraków, too, nestles beside a fawn in the Berkeley hills; there are shades of Dante on a Miwok trail, and Wang-wei haunts the slopes of Grizzly Peak.

So much is reflected and refracted here: streams of poems finding their way in the great metaphoric watershed of our listening, "bound," in the Kenneth Rexroth line that ends this book, on their "long recurrent cycle from the sky to the sea."

—*Murray Silverstein for Sixteen Rivers Press*
Oakland, November 2009

This Air

Land's End

This air,
you say, *feels as if it hasn't touched land*
for a thousand miles,

as surf sound washes through scrub
and eucalyptus,
whether ocean or wind in the trees

or both: the park's big windmill
turning overhead
while joggers circle the ball field

only a few yards off
this path secreted in growth and mist,
the feel of a long narrow theater set

about it here on the park's western edge
just in from the highway
then the moody swells of the Pacific.

The way the chill goes out of us
and the sweat comes up
as we drive back into the heat

and how I need to take you
to all the special places, or show
you where the fog rolls down

and breaks apart in these hills or where
that gorgeous little piano bridge
comes halfway through the song,

because when what has become dormant,
meager or hardened
passes through the electric

of you, the fugitive scattered pieces
are called back to their nature—
light pouring through muslin

in a strange, bare room.

from **An Atlas of the Difficult World**

Within two miles of the Pacific rounding
this long bay, sheening the light for miles
inland, floating its fog through redwood rifts and over
strawberry and artichoke fields, its bottomless mind
returning always to the same rocks, the same cliffs, with
ever-changing words, always the same language
—this is where I live now.   If you had known me
once, you'd still know me now though in a different
light and life.   This is no place you ever knew me.

But it would not surprise you
to find me here, walking in fog, the sweep of the great ocean
eluding me, even the curve of the bay, because as always
I fix on the land.   I am stuck to earth.   What I love here
is old ranches, leaning seaward, lowroofed spreads between rocks
small canyons running through pitched hillsides
liveoaks twisted on steepness, the eucalyptus avenue leading
to the wrecked homestead, the fogwreathed heavy-chested cattle
on their blond hills.   I drive inland over roads
closed in wet weather, past shacks hunched in the canyons
roads that crawl down into darkness and wind into light
where trucks have crashed and riders of horses tangled
to death with lowstruck boughs.   These are not the roads
you knew me by.   But the woman driving, walking, watching
for life and death, is the same.

Balance

Soon after I moved to California
I felt tremors everywhere. It made for
headaches and a vivid idea of how
delicately each thing was balanced,
bird upon sky, sky upon roof, roof
upon post & lintel. What trees I saw
had shifted in the sockets towards the
sky, some hanging loose and some
undressed by fire until black, wire-tipped,
and deaf. The heat loosened from
the ruptured earth was the same heat
I felt once leaving the surgery room—
with one eye cut I saw things as a
fish does. A flat world, pulled
in all directions by this tremendous
current that sets down the world's
balance, aligns people with doors
and throws me off the sidewalk,
a tremor of mind: in less than a small
touch I crumple down, and the tea
I am holding is immersed in the
puddles, and my body turns
the waters fragrant.

Waterwheel

I sat with slivers of foxtails in each sock
And a stick that stirred rainwater,
Gush of a cloud that passed over our house.
I was five. It was five in the afternoon,
Spring I guess. The mailman had come and gone
On his bicycle, his pants gnashed in the oily chain.
The diesels had stopped. The whistle at Sun-Maid Raisin
Had cleared the air. Men the color of sparrows
Had walked home, father among them, all tired
And swinging their lunch pails like lanterns.
I was coming alive. Sure, I was cold,
And my shoes were curled. Sure, my hair was wet
And I was beginning to shiver. But I was waiting
For Arnold, a boy up the alley. He promised
Me the Chinese garden in a clam shell—
Waterwheel, bridge, and a woman with a fan,
Quiet beauty on a street stomped all night by machinery.
I waited with rain on my eyelashes.
Fortune was mine. After all, hadn't I raced my bicycle
Under a moving diesel? Hadn't I pushed myself
Hand over fist on the telephone wire?
I waited for the Chinese garden
And its waterwheel to turn in the long life of rain.

Where bushes periodically burn, children fear other children: girls

whose scornings are flint on dry rock
which—don't we know—is all the heart afforded
a certain type: untended, magnifying boys.

oh fickle lens! oh smoke and smoldering beetle!
oh thwarted desire in foothills of brush
and now flame.

Wildfire Season

West Marin, California

When we were lovers, everything
reminded me of sex. Not just the usual
phallic fruits or the labia of flowers but the pulse
above your collar as I watched you drive.
My hands handing you anything,
book or butter knife. In my palm loose change
still warm from your hip pocket.

And when we said we would always be friends,
everything reminded me of sex. Our last
walk along Drake's Beach like a riptide—
pelicans swaggering through the sky
in macho gangs flaunting their long bills, great
bulbed strands of kelp swimming in high tide rills
toward cliffs flush with sunset,

the way I opened to you later
on our way home in the dark so hot
we didn't stop to lay down jacket or sweater
but ground ourselves into dry grass and gravel
on the slope above the pullout, didn't stop
at the sounds of other night animals scrabbling
in the brush around us, our motion
frozen only in the strobe of passing headlights.

So hot I remember thinking it was wildfire
season, and we should have stayed near water.
Though maybe it was better this way,
the possibility of the grass going up all at once—
we'd never know what hit us.
Like the wild hare frozen in your headlights' shaft
that very dusk—no time to swerve.

Back from the Fields

Until nightfall my son ran in the fields,
looking for God knows what.
Flowers, perhaps. Odd birds on the wing.
Something to fill an empty spot.
Maybe a luminous angel
or a country girl with a secret dark.
He came back empty-handed,
or so I thought.

Now I find them:
thistles, goatheads
the barbed weeds
all those with hooks or horns
the snaggle-toothed, the grinning ones
those wearing lantern jaws
old ones in beards, leapers
in silk leggings, the multiple
pocked moons and spiny satellites, all those
with juices and saps
like the fingers of thieves
nation after nation of grasses
that dig in, that burrow, that hug winds
and grab handholds
in whatever lean place.

It's been a good day.

The Laden Henceforth Pending

My assignment was *one useful plan,*
to make one useful plan of the surrounding
thirteen hundred acres of chaparral

and oak, manzanita and bunchgrass
in the season of the oak's unfurling,
in the season of the blue-eyed grasses,

wind-washed and rain-swept and moving
toward the scorch of summer,—*make
an afternoon of it,* he said.

Three dogs came with me up the hill
named for its sugar-pines, to what
we call the *little pike*—that farthest

meadow of my childhood,—the red head
of the vulture bent with watching,
the red tail of the hawk spread wide.

Your memory casts a shadow when you
go into the future, and the shadow
wants to know what owns you—the red

and lichened trunk of the madrona
or the twin dry creeks converging as matter
and lack of matter meeting. You have to be

nothing, take whatever amnesty is offered—
the case for love is not the case
for tragedy revisited, or there is

for certain now—a laden henceforth pending.

Peach Fires

Out in the orchards the dogs stood

Almost frozen in the bleak spring night
& Mister dragged out into the rows
Between his peach trees the old dry limbs

Building at regular intervals careful pyres
While the teeth of the dogs chattered & snapped
& the ice began to hang long as whiskers

From the globes along the branches
& at his signal we set the piles of branches ablaze
Tending each carefully so as not to scorch

The trees as we steadily fed those flames
Just enough to send a rippling glow along
Those acres of orchard where that body—

Sister Winter—had been held so wisely to the fire

Apart from Branches

Apart from branches in courtyards and small stones,
    The countryside is beyond me.
    I can go along University Avenue from Rochester to Sobrante
    And then the Avenue continues to the Bay.

    Often I think of the dry scope of foothill country,
    Moraga Hill, Andreas, Indian country, where I was born
    And where in the scrub the air tells me
    How to be born again.

    Often I think of the long rollers
    Breaking against the beaches
    All the way down the coast to the border
    On bookish cressets and culverts blue and Mediterranean.

    There I break
    In drops of spray as fine as letters
    Blown high, never to be answered,
    But waking am the shore they break upon.

    Both the dry talkers, those old Indians,
    And the dry trollers, those old pirates,
    Say something, but it's mostly louder talking,
    Gavel rapping, and procedural dismays.

    Still where we are, and where we call and call,
    The long rollers of the sea come in
    As if they lived there. The dry Santa Ana
    Sweeps up the town and takes it for a feast.

    Then Rochester to El Sobrante is a distance
    No longer than my name.

Origins

Thinking he was asking about race, I told him I was black;
and, thinking he was asking where I come from, I told him
I was from the South and from here in California and, really,
I am from the people I love who love me; and, thinking
he was asking about my sexual orientation, I told him, yes,
I am sexually oriented, especially with some men; then,
thinking he was asking about my religion, I told him I had none
to speak of except for my awe of the spirit; and, hearing
him ask specifically where I was coming from, I told him then
I come from wherever it is strangers tell their lives
in ways far less specific than speaking to each other dreams,
which is how, if I had been thinking, I should have told him
about myself.

Landmarks

My former husband had a V-shaped scar from an accident, a souvenir of the South American country his family fled to from Nazi Germany, aided by his father's employer, whose wife became his father's wife after his mother's death. The doctor, German like my husband's family but not Jewish, stitched the wound badly. It took years to embroider a tablecloth. I embroidered placemats, aprons, guest towels, then, like my mother, a tablecloth. I didn't learn until after I'd completed the green tablecloth that I should have crossed the white stitches in the same direction: I doubt my mother crossed-stitched correctly. Whatever the direction, it was satisfying to push the needle through the tough fabric and watch the stitches form diverse, unrecognizable patterns. Hoops, first wooden, then metal, held the fabric taut. I've gone back to the piano; Joyce Carol Oates also plays the piano. As I try to sleep I hunt for, then find, the name of the man who didn't answer my letters asking for a job; his replacement, after his death, didn't answer either. I was to recognize my college friend who'd moved here by her Citroën, but when I drove around Golden Gate Park there was no Citroën, no friend. She was studying dance the next time we spoke during a visit to the university town across-country she had moved back to, where my son was attending the college we'd attended, where I'd conceived the baby stillborn in the West. His scar on the inside of his arm at the bend of the elbow was preternaturally white and slightly puckered; if it had been on his face he'd have looked like a criminal. Does my friend still play piano like an artist—Joyce Carol Oates and I play Chopin, I still like a novice. Again she's moved here and this time we'll attend the wedding of another classmate so we'll finally meet. Since she's chosen the West again, I consider its merits: I'm here with my books, my manuscripts and my childhood piano—but my home, which is my history, is elsewhere.

Esta Noche

In a dress with a black tulip's sheen
      la fabulosa Lola enters, late, mounts the stairs
to the plywood platform, and begs whoever runs
      the wobbling spot to turn the lights down

to something flattering. When they halo her
      with a petal-toned gel, she sets to haranguing,
shifting in and out of two languages like gowns
      or genders to *please* have a little respect

for the girls, flashing the one entrancing
      and unavoidable gap in the center of her upper teeth.
And when the cellophane drop goes black,
      a new spot coronas her in a wig

fit for the end of a century,
      and she tosses back her hair—risky gesture—
and raises her arms like a widow in a blood tragedy,
      all will and black lace, and lipsyncs "You and Me

against the World." She's a man
      you wouldn't look twice at in street clothes,
two hundred pounds of hard living, the gap in her smile
      sadly narrative—but she's a monument,

in the mysterious permission of the dress.
      This is Esta Noche, a Latin drag bar in the Mission,
its black door a gap in the face
      of a battered wall. All over the neighborhood

storefront windows show all night
      shrined hats and gloves, wedding dresses,
First Communion's frothing lace:
      gowns of perfection and commencement,

fixed promises glowing. In the dress
    the color of the spaces between streetlamps
Lola stands unassailable, the dress
    in which she is in the largest sense

fabulous: a lesson, a criticism and colossus
    of gender, all fire and irony. Her spine's
perfectly erect, only her fluid hands moving
    and her head turned slightly to one side.

She hosts the pageant, Wednesdays and Saturdays,
    and men come in from the streets, the trains,
and the repair shops, lean together to rank
    the artifice of the awkward or lovely

Lola welcomes onto the stage: Victoria, Elena,
    Francie, lamé pumps and stockings and always
the rippling night pulled down over broad shoulders
    and flounced around the hips, liquid,

the black silk of esta noche
    proving that perfection and beauty are so alien
they almost never touch. Tonight, she says,
    put it on. The costume is license

and calling. She says you could wear the whole damn
    black sky and all its spangles. It's the only night
we have to stand on. Put it on,
    it's the only thing we have to wear.

April in San José

In a city where men shout across the streets
Shit Shit   God bless you lady   ay Miguel
bark wordless pain like dogs
roar rage in one dark syllable
or stand and beat an oak tree with their fists
or walk ten feet of driveway back and forth
in boots and Nazi cap and steel chains
or sit and shiver, silent, in the sun,

I steer among the wrecks, the reefs,

through poppies, roses, red valerian,
passionflower, trumpetvine,
camellia, dogwood, foam of plum and pear,
mock orange and true orange,
gold of the Hesperides,
sweetness of freesias, garlands, wreaths
of red and yellow, white and green,
dark fragrance of eucalyptus,
glitter and rustle of inordinate palms.

Through the mockingbird morning
I make my way bewildered
in the city of ruined men
in the valley of the ghosts of orchards
in the broken heart of California
in the nation of addiction
in the kindest month.

One Bright Morning

for Loren Chandler, 1937–2006

Freeway traffic was stopped dead
so I followed the river road.
Hay trucks crawled south to Ryer Island
as balers in the fields pulled drying
alfalfa into the front end and dumped out
fresh bales behind. West, Mount Diablo,
then the Delta spread before me,
the Delta you loved to the end.
It was a glorious morning, and I stopped
to take a memorial piss in the snakegrass
and salute the breeze riffling the water's
blue skin. A man dropped traps
along the slough. I found myself taking
the crawdad's side—no traps!—all quarry
left behind. I couldn't see anything
detained on a morning like this.
The landscape gathered into our last trip—
sheep with new lambs, Canada geese, great
blue heron climbing the air like old men.
Last time I saw you, sinking into your bed,
it was morning, bright, promise of noonday heat.
Hours after I was gone, you were gone.
Simple as that. "One bright morning,"
goes the song, "I'll fly away."
Forgive the hymn, friend. Out of doors
it doesn't count as praying.

The Poem for Gonzales, California

for Tony Doyle

Gonzales will always be
a cold, clear night
in early March, a place
on Highway 101
between Soledad and Salinas
where, returning late
from a trip to Santa Barbara,
I chose to pull off the road
and drive into a field,
exhausted, sick in soul,
halfway to divorce and as sure
of my own death as I was
of the sour milk taste
coating the inside of my mouth.
When I switched off the engine
I heard the breathing
of my two small daughters
asleep in the back seat,
and knew that they would
continue on without me,
that the world would,
with no fanfare and less
concern.

      A deep quiet
settled around the car.
The dark field encircled me.
The stars, a glittering panorama
through the windshield, ticked
across the sky. I was more alone
than I had ever been,
and didn't know
where that realization
would lead me.

             Shut in that car—
an insect in his carapace
surrounded by the field
and the endless, inching
movement of the stars—
I listened to the breathing
from the back seat, knowing
that whatever I decided
would determine
the rest of my life.
Ten minutes later
I flipped on the ignition
and drove toward home.

             This happened
in Gonzales, California,
a town that a friend now tells me
has been taken off the map.
It happened in a field
I could never find again
but have marked on my memory
as the place at my back
I start from and continue on.

Wally Watch

Brother what's that go for?
Is what I said to the man so far ahead he was behind
Behind the present time
Which I didn't understand you see, because he was in the business of
knowing
He sold timepieces
Called him Wally Watch
Sold knockoff Rolexes on the corner of Broadway and Kearny
A sinner's block
While he watched time expire over North Beach
He'd seen the sun stumble on low-set fog
Running to the islands off the coast of the city
A time or two
An evening or three
One week turned into a lifetime
Watching all the forgotten queens
In Cinderella clear plastic spiked slippers
Stroll, strut, and slide down silver college tuition poles
Paid out by the prep-school punks one district down
One for one fifty!
Or two for two!
I'm in the business of time
And I got the time for you
But just give me a second brother
Wally rapped back
While in the middle of a monologue on Swiss movement
And since I was in the middle of hurrying up to slow down
I took the time to listen
And watched Wally Watch gab with precision
Underneath neon lights, black lights
And Mac masks of tricking and fornication
I sat back and took in
A hustler's education

Patterson Pass

This is the place that inhabits us,
the place where inversion, layering down,
spills water into trough and tap of valley—

Altamont of my rib, aqueduct of your chest
        anchor of homes, totem of tract and sky
        tied up in blue's drawstring bag

below me you   and sky above   all that dihedral flight
distilled down to seep-spring monkey flower.

This landscape has settled into a familiar refrain:
        kestrel   kite   shrike   redtail
        folding into the blade
        sometimes a crow

Sometimes a man saying *hey*: an exhalation.

Here, uncertainty does not seem complex,
        loaded as it is onto crackling pallets
        and driven off to sub-stations of the west.

Wind, and how we don't understand the farming of it
how the mills hum, moan, susurrate hoarsely,
how the skin cartwheels into windmills,
electromagnetic field.

Nor the houndstooth scoring of riparian beds.
Nor the sleek catwalk of girder.

We can't see the tomorrow-land of here,
only a cow's four feet
plugged into the hills.

Rattlesnake

*"... some men were going around hunting ... and they found a big cave,
and as they were entering it they discovered a great rattlesnake coiled up
which had its face larger than the face of a cat. ..."*

ASCENSION SOLORSANO, *the last fluent native speaker
of the Mutsun language, who died in Gilroy in 1930*

The snake was in its cave, dreaming of rats,
its tongue tasting the air,
key-slot eyes open on the dark corridor of itself,
when the hunters stumbled on it
thickly coiled, a pool of snake.
Its rattles hissed once,
but their guns shot its head off
and that was the end of the snake.
They cut off its rattles as a keepsake.

The ants came looking and the hunters
left. Yet the sound it had made—
a fierce blast of sand in an empty bucket—
stayed in their ears,
and they walked all night in terror,
tramping coils.

The snake flattened in death and bled out its history.
Out rushed the winters that once held it hostage,
the summer mornings when it poured itself downhill
to bask on a flat ledge.
The sun's hand on its long, long back
traveled warm like a train through a tunnel.
Fast to strike, slow to swallow,
the snake would eye whatever moved.

Rattlesnake, I speak to your dust
in homage. Ancient one of the flatiron face,
the ominous repose,
who but you could know so well
the skin of the mountain?
Who but you was its lover?

Bronze Horse Cast from Driftwood—Do Not Touch

Deborah Butterfield's sculpture stands in the foyer
of the Cantor Gallery, Stanford, California

These are the trees the wind blew down.
This is the wood that rivers washed away
and waves brought back.

These are the limbs scattered and collected

This is the mind and these are the hands.

This is the clay casing. This is the wood burned away
and this the metal sputtering into the mold.
These are the ashes brushed away
and the metal has turned to branches.

These are trees recollected in metal, purged to their effigies, shaken free of themselves,
    swept up
into horse.

This is the horse recollected
in branches lashing in the mane, the tail, the belly.
This is the horse of the hands, of water, wind and metal,
this is the horse standing, lifelike
(in the mind the dead stand like this)
turning to look

This is the horse turning to look, to bite at a fly, so lifelike
a notch for the eye, so lifelike,
how can you bear not to touch?

Lighthouse

From the charred remains of the Vision Fire—*we see*

As we believe—a green scar implicating us in earthly affairs

Green land grab of coyote bush and cow parsnip

Flourishing without vengeance where Paradise Estates once stood

Bishop pine growing into conflagrations

Cones detonating from sealed pitch—exploding shells

Seeds tearing open ground in a bright wound—

We were driving, sucked in by the ocean's breath

Into clouds and crowds of salt-slaked pine

Green burned in us—tourist dollars

Wolves to the flock, realtors to the vista point—

We were talking—words were waters in far-off deserts

Falling into oil fires, indiscriminately

We were looking—trees grew intricate in passages of the brain

We imagined being—before we were—

In briny intertidal zones—pliant among rushes

Whelmed with light spent in the estranged light of day

Shuddering

Back to This

Coastline

Sequoia

Gothic towers of needles in the valley of a stream
not far from Mount Tamalpais where in the morning and
evening thick fog comes like the wrath and passion of the ocean

in this reservation of giants they display a cross-section of a tree
                                        the coppery stump of the West
with immense regular veins like rings on water
and someone perverse has inscribed the dates of human history
an inch from the middle of the stump the fire of a distant Rome
                                        under Nero
in the middle of the battle of Hastings the night expedition of the
                                        drakkars
panic of the Anglo-Saxons the death of the unfortunate Harold
it is told with a compass
and finally right next to the beach of the bark the landing of the
                                        Allies in Normandy

the Tacitus of this tree was a geometrician and he did not know
                                        adjectives
he did not know syntax expressing terror he did not know any words
therefore he counted added years and centuries as if to say there is
                                        nothing
beyond birth and death nothing only birth and death
and inside the bloody pulp of the sequoia

Her Flag

On one of our long, wearing walks
down the dirt path fronting the length
and breadth of our patch of ocean,
back from Sunset
Nursery—me only half-kiddingly griping,
sorely hobbling on
                         the ankle sprained
at racquetball three months before,
and she, heartily, as is her way, more than half-
mockingly laughing me silly, laughing our loony
heads off . . . As good as it gets.

While kvetching, I'm schlepping a sack of compost soil;
Naomi cradles and shades a potted, dancing-doll-legged
cymbidium orchid in her arms, white fluttering
blossoms, delectable yellow centers, edged
shell-pink membrane translucent as a newborn's
eyelid, her open hand shields; the same hand
at the mom-and-pop grocery will pick the battered
bruised fruit and vegetables because no one else will.

With our swaying matching swag and all her gangling
angles softened with delight, each curl and petal—part
vein, part flame—in range of the ocean's terrestrial
                                              erasure . . .
     We have bought, she and I, a piece
                         of the same action.

Golden Hat

STEFANIE MARLIS

The insects are living their short summer lives
as castanets, tambourines. We see it coming, the thing
we know is certain. At a crosswalk, the dream—
unsteady hand holding the rim of a golden hat.

Florid clouds tipped toward the ocean,
Johnny Appleseed clouds, a friend calls down
from an upstairs window, a light coming on in her mouth
as if a match were struck.

Peter, there's a people who believe you go on
until the very last one who's heard about you is gone.

                              for Peter Marlis

california poppy

shuddering back to this coastline, craggy old goat rock
or the sweep of dune where judah meets squid-ink pacific
no more the nomad for now.   or—stubbornly—everywhere, as each
exotic dancer filling the cracked sidewalks of north beach

as the indigent waving his tattered placard on the island
[what we call this meridian near church & dolores where the fronds
of palmtrees are stippled with shrill green or yellow lorikeets]
saying "come to my island: live cast-off cargo on this desolate reef"

—as the transmissible fruitfly larvae ravaging local oranges
as a fragile head upon a thinning stalk that somehow manages
to clasp hands at evening and send up its muttering entreaty
so small you might not notice, so ubiquitous, you see

so many ugly little flapping faces pocking city car lots,
the freeway onramps, the piss-scented flowerpots,
the unclaimed and untended plots (so few—and yet they're dense
with the wispy strands of hair and the folds of sallow tents)

that you've your right to ignore them, to ignore the grasping
fingers and bloated waxy face of the wildly surviving thing
that once was somebody's boutonnière, somebody's flash of light,
trail of phosphorescent streetlamps punctuating the homeless night

The Aftermath

And in spring poppies splayed from ash and seed
the city sprayed onto the fragile steeps.

Scorched foundations, concrete burnt
strangely pink, bereft even of mudsill—hosted

swimming poppies as did the hills
anywhere hose could stretch. Tradesmen

swam among them. Megaliths
of blackened chimneys, useless,

shedding new shadows; fence posts burned away
inside their concrete holes. Things sifting down

as the houses collapsed, fiery wall
to smoking floor to ground.

A mass of pennies, hidden like a nest
in the filth, its bowl and bureau gone.

A tray of silver, half articulate, half molten.
Sooted coins. A coat hook. A gutted house

demolished to build a house. House that
after seconds, the bulldozer rested

atop a pile of sticks, having crashed
through the dining room, and lifted the roof

off with its bucket. Then circling—with a tap,
folded each of the outer walls in. And tracking

the wreck to reduce its bulk, disturbed a nest
of bees that straggled out—lifted, and streamed

buzzing, furiously circling the abandoned
dozer, their sweetness stolen, lost, and

confused or alert to what had ruined them
—alighted—parading the yellow metal bulk,

wings spread upon air.

Oakland–Berkeley Hills Fire, 1991

California Coast

The Ohlone walk among us, setting fire to the stipa;
their fields of vast burning among the freeways

and condominiums deposit ash upon the sand
upon the decaying shells of white sand clam,

the many littleneck clams. *Holy Mary, mother of God
the Lord is with thee,* the catechumens chant

as they march around the mission chapel. Father Serra
proselytizes among the clapper rails, the furious

scrub jays, as seams open in the sidewalks and visionaries
come forth, singing of fishes and loaves, planets aligned,

Rahjneesh, Eckankar (we will consume anything: snakes,
God). The Pomo still eat the chiton, chew the tough

flesh, discarding the sandy carapace. It is said
Jaime de Angulo plowed his ledge of land 2000 ft.

above Torre Canyon in his all-together. Died sad
and crazy, having lost his European manners

and his son to the rubbled cliffs. I know
there is a rocky ledge beyond which all things

fall away; the ground shudders beneath our beds
and we prick up like frightened ground squirrels

hearing a sound like the Southern Pacific about to derail
in the front yard. Now and then, one of us plunges

into the starry field of excess and awe.

A Cone of the Eucalyptus

(San Rafael, for Mark Solomon)

So many piled beneath the peeling tree
it seems a late polluted hail had come,
some antediluvian, post-biblical plague
that fell and fell and blotted out the sun
and would not melt, but scattered like leaves

across the walk where you bend down, pick one,
then place it squarely in my palm. "Look, Dan,
at the star-shape on the crown, the hollow cone
a bloom of five born out of four." And soon
you're quoting sages—Plato and Thomas Browne—

"the quincunx blossoming from quaternity":
such mystical symmetries, to which you add
bodies in the Kaballah, the Tarot, the Torah,
Christ on the Cross, snowflakes, the human hand.
I run my thumb along the pith. Four scars

ascend to where something—call it nature—
fixed hull to crest, each rough plane perfected
like a fossil browned by centuries in earth,
and five carved points that open into black,
and look like a seal, and are deeply cured.

Mark, my *reb*, whose name doubles wisdom,
you could convince me to believe in Blake
and his eternity, a heaven encased in words;
this shell the image my own soul might make,
its wounds at seed under bone-white boughs.

16th & Valencia

I saw Jack Micheline reciting Skinny Dynamite
on the corner of 16th & Valencia
and he was angry
and the next day he was dead on the last BART train to Concord
and maybe that's why he was angry
I met Harold Norse shuffling around in a beaten world
his pockets stuffed with poems only hipsters read
It's a cesspool out here he sighed
before retreating to his room in the Albion Hotel
where angels honeycomb the walls with dreams
and the rent is paid with angry poems
I heard Oscar Zeta Acosta's brown buffalo footsteps
pounding the Valencia Corridor
and he was shouting poetry at the sick junkies
nodding with their wasted whores
in the lobby of the Hotel Royan "The Mission's finest"
and even the furniture was angry
I joined the waiters at the bus stop
the waitresses the norteños trios the flower sellers
the blind guitarist wailing boleros at a purple sky
the shirtless vagrant vagabond ranting at a parking meter
the spray paint visionary setting fire to the word
and I knew this was the last call
We were tired of living from the scraps of others
We were tired of dying for our own chunk of nothing
And I saw this barrio as a freight train
a crazy Mexican bus careening out of control
a mutiny aboard a battleship
and every porthole filled with anger
And we were going to stay angry
And we were not leaving
Not ever leaving
El corazón del corazón de La Misión
El Camino Real ends here

He walked through the roughest part of town with an armload of flowers

Steamboat iron ferry puffing huffing
turning a wide arc against a muscular
tide in the carved strait late-afternoon
whitecaps snap crack glad cold
north sea memories—happy then
to walk hard narrow streets of
foul tenements piled up behind the
waterfront canning sheds, docks,
derricks and wreckage, steep and
crooked the wayward cobbles,
dingy laundry hanging limp, him
besieged by a swirl of grimy-
faced mugginses holding out their
blackened hands begging a single
sun-bright blossom picked on sweet
treeless slopes across the bay far away
his brown coat muddy boots slouch hat
so many brilliant red and yellow stars
balanced atop green wands their lightning
flashing in the eyes, the glassless windows
of the other paradise, constellations shining
over the sills of small fouled rooms
his old worn corduroy dusted with gold.

Two Mexicanos Lynched in
Santa Cruz, California, May 3, 1877

More than the moment
when forty *gringo* vigilantes
cheered the rope
that snapped two *Mexicanos*
into the grimacing sleep of broken necks,

more than the floating corpses,
trussed like cousins of the slaughterhouse,
dangling in the bowed mute humility
of the condemned,

more than the *Virgen de Guadalupe*
who blesses the brownskinned
and the crucified,
or the guitar-plucking skeletons
they will become
on the *Dia de los Muertos,*

remain the faces of the lynching party:
faded as pennies from 1877, a few stunned
in the blur of execution,
a high-collar boy smirking, some peering
from the shade of bowler hats, but all
crowding into the photograph.

The J Car

Last year I used to ride the J CHURCH Line,
Climbing between small yards recessed with vine
—Their ordered privacy, their plots of flowers
Like blameless lives we might imagine ours.
Most trees were cut back, but some brushed the car
Before it swung round to the street once more
On which I rolled out almost to the end,
To 29th Street, calling for my friend.

    He'd be there at the door, smiling but gaunt,
To set out for the German restaurant.
There, since his sight was tattered now, I would
First read the menu out. He liked the food
In which a sourness and dark richness meet
For conflict without taste of a defeat,
As in the Sauerbraten. What he ate
I hoped would help him to put on some weight,
But though the crusted pancakes might attract
They did so more as concept than in fact,
And I'd eat his dessert before we both
Rose from the neat arrangement of the cloth,
Where the connection between life and food
Had briefly seemed so obvious if so crude.
Our conversation circumspectly cheerful,
We had sat here like children good but fearful
Who think if they behave everything might
Still against likelihood come out all right.

    But it would not, and we could not stay here:
Finishing up the Optimator beer
I walked him home through the suburban cool
By dimming shape of church and Catholic school,
Only a few white teenagers about.
After the four blocks he would be tired out.
I'd leave him to the feverish sleep ahead,
Myself to ride through darkened yards instead
Back to my health. Of course I simplify.

Of course. It tears me still that he should die
As only an apprentice to his trade,
The ultimate engagements not yet made.
His gifts had been withdrawing one by one
Even before their usefulness was done:
This optic nerve would never be relit;
The other flickered, soon to be with it.
Unready, disappointed, unachieved,
He knew he would not write the much-conceived
Much-hoped-for work now, nor yet help create
A love he might in full reciprocate.

Death Looks Down

Death looks down on the salmon.
A male and a female in two pools, one above
the other. The female turns back along the path
of water to the male, does not touch him,
and returns to the place she had been.

I know what death will do. Their bodies already
are sour and ragged. Blood has risen
to the surface under the scales. One side
of his jaw is unhinged. Death will pick them up.
Put them under his coat against his skin
and belt them in there. Will walk away
up the path through the bay trees.
Through the dry grass of California to where
the mountain begins. Where a few deer
almost the color of the hills will look up
until he is under the trees again and the road ends
and there is a gate. He will climb over that
with his treasure. It will be dark by then.

But for now he does nothing. He does not disturb
the silence at all. Nor the occasional sound
of leaves, of ferns touching, of grass or stream.
For now he looks down at the salmon large and whole
motionless days and nights in the cold water.
Lying still, always facing the constant motion.

Confluence

To the San Joaquin River

Too-warm trickler,
old sand pit,
it can't afford
salmon.
It's been bifurcated,
sand-and-gravelled,
canalled and cancelled.
One hundred fifty miles
of has-been
below the dam
that uses it up,
almost,
bends it out of course.
We're all spent rivers,
one time or another,
pooling where we can
to reflect the willows
and the graffitied bridge
as we search our way
down toward the confluence.

Blue-Black

That road leads only
to the bridge, to the
hiss and slap
of water, the muddy
suck of the bottom.
I know the way.

All winter
I pitched through night in a fury of falling,
falling,
wind in my teeth,
my body an old coat with stones
in its pockets.

I found my body on the bridge.
Fingers locked to the cold rail,
counting, as if
the blue-black
slippery ocean were a hope
to hang onto.

I knew that old coat,
the brown shag, the missing
buttons. I watched
my slow fingers
choosing. My knuckles.
My stubborn feet.

A Place to Live

Even though—both of us knowing you could die any time,
both of us *wanting* to believe when you said this would be
the place you'd come to if you could—I seldom
come here and wait on this log turned almost into stone.
Even though keeping our word was life between us, given
all *that* in trust, still I seldom walk under these trees,
redwood and eucalyptus, the branches of Monterey pine
over the path opening farther than we could see the morning
you told me you'd surely try to come. I've tried being here,
stopped and stood quiet to see if you could make it, but I'm
always either too early or too late and just miss you, in time
only for a voice that tells me living my life's a way of being
faithful. Even though the trees keep changing and love is
behind or ahead of me in the clearing I trust as I trust
this ground: the duff and dark needles underfoot, the light
through high green lace pulling the trees into the sky.

A Blessing

I had hiked to the top of the ridge and sat to rest
against a tree, under a nest, the ocean
three miles down to my left but the smell of it
up here strong and salty. Waiting for the thrush,
I looked up to a low murmur
and a house hove up out of the thicket
and two men, naked, walked across a patio to a flat rock wall
and sat, their bare feet dangling above cypress and scrub oak.
The breeze took their words but the tone was woodwind
and the one with the dark hair drawn back in a bandana
laid his cheek on the blond man just in the soft hollow
formed by the clavicle and deltoid and put his right hand
on the other's cock, pressing it between his palm
and the warm slate where it stirred like a small animal.
In the time it took for me to blink my eyes
and swallow, they rose and turned, swift and fluid,
and walked away from me, under the overhang, into the shade,
the blond man's hand on the arc of the other's buttock,
and were gone, leaving me with gooseflesh in the freshening
wind, and the poor, distant beauty of the Pacific.

The Signature Mark of Autumn

The signature mark of autumn has arrived at last with the rains: orange of pumpkin, orange persimmon, orange lichen on rocks and fallen logs; a copper moon hung low over the orchard; moist, ruddy limbs of the madrone, russet oak leaf, storm-peeled redwood, acorns emptied by squirrels and jays; and mushrooms, orange boletes, Witch's Butter sprouting on rotted oak, the Deadly Galeria, and of course, chanterelles, which we'll eat tonight with pasta, goat cheese, and wine.

Next and the Corner

And so it was,

in such a way, like aging into my days

I had come to resemble

the dead movie house on Mission
called the El Capitán.

Three figures
at the gates of the gully,

gold March sun tinged with shadow—
as the other cars kept pulling away—

across the plain—in the hillside,

admixture of red bottle brush   and the plane overhead

three figures at the gates of the gully,

so who do tell the dead most of youth is misspent
curating a secret language,
who do tell the dead.

Fence to the fencepost,
you be lost,
you be contained.

Like One

Eternity

Touching

Another

Home from the Sierra

Woke once in the night, pissed,
checkt the coming winter's stars
built up the fire
still glowing in the chilly dawn.

Washing the mush pot in the lake
frost on the horse turds
a grayjay cased the camp.

All morning walking to the car
load up on granite stone,
seedling sugar pine.

Down to hot plains.
Mexicans on flatcars in the San Joaquin.
Cool fog
smell of straw mats
cup of green tea
by the Bay.

from **Involuntary Lyrics**

San Francisco, ah, west
of ascension, none of us wanted posterity
before we got to pleasure it! Another
sick, sickening, the
last newest
in his prime.
You, for all of us came crawling through dim alleys to mother
and shining see
even if still we're trailing in and out of city's womb
calls us and too discharges time
alone inside our tender bodies—dry,
do, my still-seeing eyes; nightmare's made me raise my fearful head again. Be
extravagant meaningful polis, clearful sky, the
really it has been loving gesture of light undoes the tomb!

Facing West from California's Shores

Facing west, from California's shores,
Inquiring, tireless, seeking what is yet unfound,
I, a child, very old, over waves, towards the house of maternity, the land
    of migrations, look afar,
Look off the shores of my Western Sea—the circle almost circled;
For, starting westward from Hindustan, from the vales of Kashmere,
From Asia—from the north—from the God, the sage, and the hero,
From the south—from the flowery peninsulas, and the spice islands,
Long having wander'd since—round the earth having wander'd,
Now I face home again—very pleas'd and joyous;
(But where is what I started for, so long ago?
And why is it yet unfound?)

Ars Poetica

Yes, the ocean is Buddhist. And the foam
scrambling onto the beach is a symphony
of cymbals, small and caring like mothers
whispering to their children in the front pew,
ssshhh. Perhaps then the trees should
believe in God. Of course. How they reach
straight up after all those years like the Chinese
grandmothers rising at dawn, when the air's
cleanest, an orchestra of their own, stretching
toward the sun. None of this true. The ocean
is only Buddhist because a poet writes of it
that way—just like the grandmothers who keep
surfacing in his poems, usually dancing
somewhere near a body of water, blissfully.

North of San Francisco

Here the soft hills touch the ocean
like one eternity touching another
and the cows grazing on them
ignore us, like angels.
Even the scent of ripe melon in the cellar
is a prophecy of peace.

The darkness doesn't war against the light,
it carries us forward
to another light, and the only pain
is the pain of not staying.

In my land, called holy,
they won't let eternity be:
they've divided it into little religions,
zoned it for God-zones,
broken it into fragments of history,
sharp and wounding unto death.
And they've turned the tranquil distances
into a nearness twitching with the pain of the present.

On the beach at Bolinas, at the foot of the wooden steps,
I saw some girls lying face-down in the sand
naked and unashamed, drunk
on the kingdom everlasting,
their souls like doors
closing and opening,
closing and opening inside them
to the rhythm of the surf.

Practical Water

What does it mean to live a moral life

It is nearly impossible to think about this

We went down to the creek
The sides were filled
    with tiny watery activities

The mind was split & mended
Each perception divided into more

& there were in the hearts of the water molecules
    little branches perpendicular to thought

Had lobbied the Congress but it was dead
Had written to the Committee on Understanding
Had written to the middle
    middle of the middle
    class but it was drinking
Had voted in cafes with shoplifters &
    beekeepers stirring tea made of water
    hitched to the green arc

An ethics occurs at the edge
of what we know

The creek goes underground about here

The spirits offer us a world of origins
Owl takes its call from the drawer of the sky

Unusually warm global warming day out

A tiny droplet shines
    on a leaf & there your creek is found

It has borrowed something to
   link itself to others

We carry ourselves through the days in code
DNA like Raskolnikov's staircase neither
   good nor bad in itself

Lower frequencies *are* the mind
What happened to the creek
   is what happened
   to the sentence in the twentieth century
It got social underground

You should make yourself uncomfortable
If not you who

Thrush comes out from the cottony
   coyote bush glink-a-glink
         chunk drink
   trrrrrr
   turns a golden eyebrow to the ground

We run past the plant that smells like taco sauce

Recite words for water
   weeter wader weetar vatn
   watn voda
[insert all languages here]

Poor Rimbaud didn't know how to live
   but knew how to act
Red-legged frog in the pond sounds like him

Uncomfortable & say a spell:
blossom knit & heel affix
fiddle fern in the neck of the sun

It's hard to be water
    to fall from faucets with fangs
    to lie under trawlers as horizons
    but you must

Your species can't say it
You have to do spells & tag them

Uncomfortable & act like you mean it

Go to the world
Where is it
Go there

The Song Mt. Tamalpais Sings

This is the last place. There is nowhere else to go.

> Human movements,
> but for a few,
> are Westerly.
> Man follows the Sun.

This is the last place. There is nowhere else to go.

> Or follows what he thinks to be the
> movement of the Sun.
> It is hard to feel it, as a rider,
> on a spinning ball.

This is the last place. There is nowhere else to go.

> Centuries and hordes of us,
> from every quarter of the earth,
> now piling up,
> and each wave going back
> to get some more.

This is the last place. There is nowhere else to go.

> "My face is the map of the Steppes,"
> she said, on this mountain, looking West.

> My blood set singing by it,
> to the old tunes,
> Irish, still,
> among these Oaks.

Art Wong Is Alive and Ill and Struggling in Oakland, California

I.
Chi Pai Shih was born
in the Year of the Boar.
And a bore he was;
his footprints dirtied the snow.

Thirty, I painted landscapes;
forty, insects and flowers;
fifty, I turned lazy as mud,
never ventured beyond
West Borrowed Hill.

II.
Oh, Nonsense! Art
is a balding painter, humpbacked
as the dwarfed acacia
dying in his father's chopsuey joint.

His palette is muddy; his thoughts are mud.
He sits crosslegged,
one eye open, the other shut,
a drunken Buddha.

I laugh at the sun; I take in air;
I whistle in sleep, let cicadas within
murmur their filial rapture.
My father's dream is my dream:
fast cars and California gold;
the singles bar is my watering hole.

III.
And I . . . I am in love with him.
Never ask why, for youth
never begs the question.
As long as boughs are green
so is my love green and pure
in this asphalt loneliness.

I let down my long hair;
my hair falls over his shoulders:
thus, we become one. Oh, Willow,
Cousin Willow, don't weep for me now.
Consummate this marriage between
Art and me, between
the diaspora and the yearning sea.

Seen from the Miwok Trail

Marin Headlands

We see it all the time
out back—the thin
break in the brush; the dusty line
cut in the ridge as if God had run a thumb-
nail across it. Hyden figures
if we walk it we can see someone waving
from the deck. So today, we drape
a large snow leopard named Maya
over the back railing
and drive to the trailhead.

Space-struck on the open ridge,
at first we cannot find
where we live;
then scarcely recognize
the tiny yellow house that appears
oddly foreign. We point
and point, but Hyden cannot find it
until—with a shout—
he waves to a white snow leopard moving amidst the green
cypress. Now I remember
the Rousseau that hung on my bedroom wall
all those boyish years. Now
it looks like
home.

Hiking Through What Remains of the Mt. Vision Fire

Amid bird calls and the wild wheat, water runs.
Raspberry and mint poke through the afternoon,
Miner's lettuce and thistle—somebody's feast.
Blue ceanothus above sword fern—I could go on.
Beyond, the ocean is calling, but not to me.

It was the white heads of hemlock I followed
up this trail, trying to recall something essential
but it eludes me. For years I refused to return
to the heat-blasted branches and scarred stone
above Limantour—so many trees felled by fire.

From the root of the Old Western, we heard
the roar of oak and eucalyptus, explosions
of cypress and pine as a rim of crimson burned
through billows of black smoke. Salt-laden—
how could they be lighter than air?

We counted buckets of water drawn
from Tomales Bay. They looked like rescue.
It was all we could do. In the saloon downstairs,
perhaps this sounded like celebration—within
the groans of each explosion, a misconceived joy—

the same jukebox songs that played on better days
adrift on the fumes of beer, the same hills dusk-lit
with coyote brush, the impossible lupine, and
the voices of children on the wind. But someone's
playing jacks in the heart's ash. Eleven years have passed.
Here and there, a white snag looms above all that is green.

Gift

A day so happy.
Fog lifted early, I worked in the garden.
Hummingbirds were stopping over honeysuckle flowers.
There was no thing on earth I wanted to possess.
I knew no one worth my envying him.
Whatever evil I had suffered, I forgot.
To think that once I was the same man did not embarrass me.
In my body I felt no pain.
When straightening up, I saw the blue sea and sails.

Berkeley, 1971

For Czesław Miłosz in Kraków

The fog has hovered off the coast for weeks
And given us a march of brilliant days
You wouldn't recognize—who have grumbled
So eloquently about gray days on Grizzly Peak—
Unless they put you in mind of puppet pageants
Your poems remember from Lithuanian market towns
Just after the First World War. Here's more theater:
A mule-tail doe gave birth to a pair of fawns
A couple of weeks ago just outside your study
In the bed of oxalis by the redwood trees.
Having dropped by that evening, I saw,
Though at first I couldn't tell what I was seeing,
A fawn, wet and shivering, curled almost
In a ball under the thicket of hazel and toyon.
I've read somewhere that does hide the young
As best they can and then go off to browse
And recruit themselves. They can't graze the juices
In the leaves if they stay to protect the newborns.
It's the glitch in engineering through which chance
And terror enter on the world. I looked closer
At the fawn. It was utterly still and trembling,
Eyes closed, possibly asleep. I leaned to smell it:
There was hardly a scent. She had licked all traces
Of the rank birth-smell away. Do you remember
This fragment from Anacreon? —the context,
Of course, was probably erotic: ". . . her gently,
Like an unweaned fawn left alone in a forest
By its antlered mother, frail, trembling with fright."
It's a verse—you will like this detail—found
In the papyrus that wrapped a female mummy
A museum in Cairo was examining in 1956.
I remember the time that a woman in Portland
Asked if you were a reader of Flannery O'Connor.
You winced regretfully, shook your head,
And said, "You know, I don't agree with the novel."
I think you haven't agreed, in this same sense,

With life, never accepted the cruelty in the frame
Of things, brooded on your century, and God the Monster,
And the smell of summer grasses in the world
That can hardly be named or remembered
Past the moment of our wading through them,
And the world's poor salvation in the word. Well,
Dear friend, you resisted. You were not mute.
Mark tells me he has seen the fawns grazing
With their mother in the dusk. Gorging on your roses—
So it seems they made it through the night
And neither dog nor car has got to them just yet.

Burnt Offerings: Mother's Day at the Lees, 1999

On Mother's Day, Dad invited the mechanic, his wife, and three
small children, to resuscitate his '76 Nova, which was the color
of a wrinkled orange and spilling more oil from every crevice
than the Exxon Valdez into the neighbors' flat calm driveways.
Dad only drove it from one side to the other to avoid street cleaners.
It was his first car, and my maternal grandmother, who died
years ago, had lent him the money to buy it. We were setting
the table with Szechwan from Mike's Chinese when the car burst
into flames. Thirty Chinese and one half-Cherokee streamed toward
the burning Nova. George, my husband, yelled at them to stop
pointing the garden hose at the gasoline fire, but everyone
screamed back in Cantonese. No one wanted to call 911.
The Chinese don't like making a scene, but it's OK
for the car to ignite other nearby cars, its flames traveling
slowly along the oil slicks. Auntie Claire suggested we pour
a box of baking soda on the fire. While Dad tried to retrieve
his stash of lucky red envelopes from the glove compartment,
twelve firefighters shattered the car windows with their axes.
Afterwards we ate. Then George and I stepped out for a smoke
and watched the neighbors celebrate the rise in property values
as the tow truck dragged away the charred hulk.

For Kenneth and Miriam Patchen

Here
I am cutting you
these fresh healthy flowers
from my sick bed
where I toss with nickel illuminations.
Time is a fever
that burns in the pores
consuming everything the mind creates.
I send you
this cool arrangement of dream blossoms
these tender stems & shiny leaves
while I shiver
& detect in your own eyes
of gentle remove
a similar disgust with what has come
to our fat cancerous land
of the sensual circus
& the disembodied broadcast wave,
swallowing in sorrow
to hear the old hatred
& uncover selfishness
rumbling back up from the bosoms of men
out into the good open air.
May these new flowers
from the forest of my heart
bring you a breath of the joy
men must believe they are going to recover
by moving again & again
against one another.

Bodhisattva West

Go ahead,
ask me if I care about
the filthy town they came to,
my great-grandfather, again a butcher,
my grandmother ashamed
of her pierced ears.

Clear across the continent,
I sit on a mountaintop
following my breath
and eyeing the vast Pacific.

Ask me if I care
that this breath first hitchhiked
across the Atlantic
inside two Polish teenagers.

What does it have to do with
this mountain laurel,
my body next to it,
dissolving,
that breath ready to leap again?

The Wild Merced

Our relentless Lady of Mercy
offers none today, makes waterfalls
from three directions across her broad
back, froth on her face,

her force carving Yosemite Valley,
rolling her rapids—Class IV and V,
in spite of Cook's cows and horses,
the railroad, sugar pine logging, dams.

I lose track of her down the thousand-foot
drop to Mariposa, lost in the highway's
descent, I don't see her veer north until I feel
the prick of winter almonds near Planada.

Before I miss her roar, I'm at the neon
Modesto Knife and Saw;
she slides noiselessly under my feet
on her way to San Pablo Bay.

Like ladder rungs from Route 49, the Merced,
Tuolumne, Mokelumne, and Stanislaus meet
the wide San Joaquin, pushing their lives
to the sea, long before the orchards with their

white painted trunks, before the first people,
before the people who conquered
those people, before gold, the sprawl
of Modesto, Turlock's blinding lights.

California, easy to lose, bound with rivers.

Feather River

You come hoping to find what you need
beneath the incense cedars
in the seaward rush of water.
Some antidote to grief.

The cautious mind refuses
new leaves from dead branches,
perfume from stones.
Look again. Look harder.

Long gazing at canyon walls,
at barn swallows in flight.
Long gazing at the blank page,
which is also sacred.

Limbs

Pieces of scenery were swaying
        left and right, an uneven spot
of branch-channeled sunlight
        being one reason we panted upslope
for the hundredth time.
        No exaggeration would make
the crunch of madrone leaves
        less ordinary, their yellow pallor
paler, their muffled scent awaken
        under the blare of bay.

Now came the time to plunge in,
        to roll on one's back under a screen
of trees golden in the last light,
        their limbs extending into
burnished air, the wind quickening
        in us a sense of being inside
some extraordinary music, reviving
        in my mind the litany of ways
I would bend, even change
        my life, if you would stay.

In a Doorway on Powell Street

I remember his stubble face,
grey eyes and white hair.

He reminded me of my grandfather
the year before he died.

His hands blindly reaching out,
gesturing to his chest.
"I'm an old man," he said. "I have a bad heart."

I started to die with him.

I gave him some money, but
not enough.

The Word That Is a Prayer

One thing you know when you say it:
all over the earth people are saying it with you;
a child blurting it out as the seizures take her,
a woman reciting it on a cot in a hospital.
What if you take a cab through the Tenderloin:
at a street light, a man in a wool cap,
yarn unraveling across his face, knocks at the window;
he says, *Please.*
By the time you hear what he's saying,
the light changes, the cab pulls away,
and you don't go back, though you know
someone just prayed to you the way you pray.
Please: a word so short
it could get lost in the air
as it floats up to God like the feather it is,
knocking and knocking, and finally
falling back to earth as rain,
as pellets of ice, soaking a black branch,
collecting in drains, leaching into the ground,
and you walk in that weather every day.

The Rainbow Grocery

You don't find it for yourself. Someone takes you.
The bars have shut down and still it is not time.
Whatever was going to happen is lost in the smoke
and the old booze, of the people who made it leaving together.
Of the quiet that comes when you've said it. Nothing to say.
That's the time of night for The Rainbow Grocery.

And it looks like nothing, like nowhere on God's earth,
like an old place abandoned. It is abandoned,
but the abandoned door opens, onto a lobby
of wax derelicts, grey as uncertain night.
No one human has sat in these chairs. No one human.
The lights are yellow and they are ready to die.

You pay a dollar to get in. Then
there's a place to check your valuables. Then
there is a dusty hall which might lead: where?
Then down a staircase to a grimy basement.
You can get coffee or soft drinks if you really want them.
That's the room where men are dancing only with men.

Past that is what it's all about: the black room.
You walk past its door and you know it's full of people,
people you can't see and were never meant to see,
hands touching you, chests, bellies, the shy night.
And if you are stripped, sucked, and the rest done to you,
The Rainbow Grocery will have taken you in.

Always at the end of a hall, of a dark hall
where there is a next room, always, a next room,
and who knows what's sleeping there, then or forever?
Always when the bars close, somebody says:
"Why don't we go down to The Rainbow Grocery?
You haven't been there? I can get you in."

As to Immortality

I'd settle for the way
that Swainson's hawk lifts off
and takes that admirable name aloft—
a single sweep of brindled wings
from the stob of a branch of a ghost of a cedar,
endlessly to sail the smooth blue folds of sky
at heights that he and his notebook never knew.

Their

Green

Flanks

Green Hills

Their green flanks
and swells are not
flesh in any sense
matching ours,
we tell ourselves.
Nor their green
breast nor their
green shoulder nor
the languor of their
rolling over.

Often I Am Permitted to Return to a Meadow

as if it were a scene made-up by the mind,
that is not mine, but is a made place,

that is mine, it is so near to the heart,
an eternal pasture folded in all thought
so that there is a hall therein

that is a made place, created by light
wherefrom the shadows that are forms fall.

Wherefrom fall all architectures I am
I say are likenesses of the First Beloved
whose flowers are flames lit to the Lady.

She it is Queen Under The Hill
whose hosts are a disturbance of words within words
that is a field folded.

It is only a dream of the grass blowing
east against the source of the sun
in an hour before the sun's going down

whose secret we see in a children's game
of ring a round of roses told.

Often I am permitted to return to a meadow
as if it were a given property of the mind
that certain bounds hold against chaos,

that is a place of first permission,
everlasting omen of what is.

The Philosopher in Golden Gate Park

To what good are words without action?
All afternoon, the hawk inviting the field mouse
from its lowly burrow with a slow cry of friendship,
false god peering down from a tree.

What else is there? A meadow resting
inside the confines of a city park
is a meadow nonetheless, and my heart
beats without so much as a single thought.

I am not an old man seeking rest,
but at times the joints ache and the mind numbs.
My mind circling the drain with questions
is numb. With so many faults, I dare not cast a stone.

Is there really such a thing as love?
The Pacific refuses to grapple with such a question.
While the wind spiraling through the dunes has no answer,
a hundred mouths open and shut in a shift of sand.

California Hills in August

I can imagine someone who found
these fields unbearable, who climbed
the hillside in the heat, cursing the dust,
cracking the brittle weeds underfoot,
wishing a few more trees for shade.

An Easterner especially, who would scorn
the meagerness of summer, the dry
twisted shapes of black elm,
scrub oak, and chaparral, a landscape
August has already drained of green.

One who would hurry over the clinging
thistle, foxtail, golden poppy,
knowing everything was just a weed,
unable to conceive that these trees
and sparse brown bushes were alive.

And hate the bright stillness of the noon
without wind, without motion,
the only other living thing
a hawk, hungry for prey, suspended
in the blinding, sunlit blue.

And yet how gentle it seems to someone
raised in a landscape short of rain—
the skyline of a hill broken by no more
trees than one can count, the grass,
the empty sky, the wish for water.

Foul Ball

The beer vendor was palming three
eighteen-ounce buckets of beer when
the ball exploded from the stretch, split-fingered,
sliding hard away from the plate, a diving
outside fastball that Santiago just couldn't
resist, so when he swung and gave it the meat
of the bat cracking against the grain the way I've heard
ice-laden limbs pop in the woods, the line drive
started out down the first-base chalk then
curved, blazing over that green stretch between
the puffed white foul line and the low
field seats, curving, coming in hard
all that new white leather massaged in
Mississippi mud just one pitch old was going
to knock twelve-fifty worth of beer
into an old guy's lap; but beer vendor
gives a quick head turn and an easy left foot
pivot like he's turning a double play
the way he's watched Aurilia give
a hundred and fifty-two times, and the ball's
coming, this inevitable foul I've waited for
in parks since I was six, and just when I reach,
the ball pops, seams on seams in the brown,
oiled glove of the kid next to me, the stitching
bulging into a smile across the web of the mitt
the same as his bright white teeth, his fist
pumping and that small voice floating deep
into straightaway center on a breeze.

The Orders

One spring night, at the end of my street
God was lying in wait.

A friend and I were sitting in his new sedan
like a couple of cops on surveillance,
shooting the breeze to pass the time,
chatting up the daydreams, the raw deals,
all the woulda-coulda-shoulda's,
the latest "Can you believe that?"
As well as the little strokes of luck,
the so-called triumphs, small and unforeseen,
that kept us from cashing it all in.

And God, who's famous for working
in mysterious ways and capable of anything,
took the form of a woman and a man,
each dressed in dark clothes and desperate enough
to walk up to the car and open the doors.

And God put a gun to the head of my friend—
right against the brain stem, where the orders go out
not only to the heart and lungs
but to consciousness itself—a cold muzzle aimed
at where the oldest urges still have their day:
the one that says eat whatever's at hand,
the one that only wants to fuck,
the one that will kill if it has to . . .

And God said not to look at him
or he'd blow us straight to kingdom come,
and God told us to keep our hands
to ourselves, as if she weren't that kind of girl.

Suddenly time was nothing,
our lives were cheap, the light in the car
cold, light from a hospital,
light from a morgue. And the moments
that followed—if that's what they were—
arrived with a nearly unbearable weight,
until we had acquired
a center of gravity
as great as the planet itself.

My friend could hardly speak—
he was too busy trying not to die—
which made me chatter all the more,
as if words, even the most ordinary ones,
had the power to return us to our lives.

And behind my ad-libbed incantation,
my counterspell to fear, the orders
still went out: keep beating, keep breathing,
you are not permitted to disappear,

even as one half of God kept bitching
to the other half that we didn't have
hardly no money at all, and the other half barked,
"I'm telling you to shut your mouth!"
and went on rummaging through the back seat.
And no one at all looking out their window,
no one coming home or going out . . .

Until two tall neighbors came walking toward us
like unsuspecting saviors . . . And God grabbed
the little we'd been given, the little we still had,
and hustled on to the next dark street.

Psalm

Veritas sequitur . . .

In the small beauty of the forest
The wild deer bedding down—
That they are there!

        Their eyes
Effortless, the soft lips
Nuzzle and the alien small teeth
Tear at the grass

        The roots of it
Dangle from their mouths
Scattering earth in the strange woods.
They who are there.

        Their paths
Nibbled thru the fields, the leaves that shade them
Hang in the distances
Of sun

        The small nouns
Crying faith
In this in which the wild deer
Startle, and stare out.

Birdsong from My Patio

Despair so easy. Hope so hard to bear.
—THOMAS MCGRATH

I've never heard this much song,
trills pure as crystal bells,
but not like bells: alive, small rushes
of air from the tiny plush lungs
of birds tucked in among the stiff
leaves of the olive and almond,
the lemon with its hard green studs.
As the sun slides down newborn
from thick-muscled clouds
their glittering voices catch the light
like bits of twirling aluminum.
I picture their wrinkled feet
curled around thin branches,
absorbing pesticide.
I see them preening, tainted
feathers sliding through their glossy
beaks, over their leathery tongues.
They're feeding on contaminated insects,
wild seeds glistening with acid rain.
And their porous, thin-shelled eggs,
bluish or milky or speckled,
lying doomed in each
intricate nest. Everything
is drenched with loss:
the wood thrush and starling,
the unripe fruit of the lemon tree.
With all that's been ruined
these songs impale the air
with their sharp, insistent needles.

Changing Forecast

Look how the sun has emerged, despite
expectations and the wringing of hands.
A new warmth rises on the April wind.

I am here again at the old crossroads: action
at odds with intention. Accomplishment sacrificed
to the short-term pleasure of just being here.

Is it so wrong to stop and reevaluate
the day's agenda? If they will pay
for the same work tomorrow, why hurry

past this hour when it all begins to make sense?
You and me, this unlikely house. Look,
the weeds have turned into forget-me-nots,

and we didn't kill the lemon after all.
Come, sit beside me and listen: I swear you can hear
the Bermuda grass growing, oak shadows deepening,

this old planet spinning on a new axis.

Piano Man

Friday night. Beautiful jazz piano at Picante's. Two people in
the room. Three grubby skateboarders and several ticket
holders waiting for their food in the next. The music, simple,
yet impossibly lovely, impossibly complicated, pours out of
the shiny black spinet. The piano player notices me listening.
He can hear me listening. He turns his head slightly to look.
I look away to avoid eye contact because the music is
impossibly intimate. How can I tell him that it's okay that no
one but me hears? That I will walk out and down Sixth Street
and he will be alone but that he must not stop playing? That
he is not alone as long as he sounds? That he means as long as
he sounds? That he cannot stop playing. He must not.

Archipelago Dust

Einstein did nothing in class but smile,
   his mind already building cities
      in grid, at sixteen. It seemed important

to learn the rules of logic and efficiency, all
   those years I posed as a student engineer.
      How numbers were always clean,

like the boys who smelled of soap, who solved
   my math problems, while I closed my eyes
      in class for minutes or hours. *Subservient circle,*

the parallelogram, unhinged. At the end of lines
   to infinity are towns lit with lost coins.
      Daydreams, I remember, while professors

gave abstractions shape. The windows were always closed:
   Manila smog tapping, the jitney's din. What a dusty
      archipelago it was. The tropical heat was the greatest ally

of the Spanish friars, kept my ancestors half-asleep.
   I only believe in stories, a friends says while
      San Francisco gets rinsed by fog. It's almost dawn,

that time when you know that everything beautiful
   about a place has nothing to do with you, and it's okay.
      Somewhere north, because they're not afraid to be thirsty

all the time, the redwoods are one breath farther from where
   they began. My friend and I eat cold fries, in our mouths
      the taste of salt and lard, the heat of drunkenness wearing off,

I tell him that in one story of belief, there's a planet
   so small a child brooms it clean in seven steps.

Wild Fennel

Two hours past spring but feeling more like winter;
cold wind tear-whipping our eyes, sun balanced
on the western hills as we stopped to see the red-winged
blackbirds where they nest in last year's reeds.

Their metallic cries and flickering red patches
saying "Here, here, I am, here"
as the wild fennel made a tunnel of the path,
brown lacey winter skeletons reached past our heads
umbrella-rib seed pods bursting like rockets in July.

I pinched a piece of the fine feathery greenness,
let you sniff the sweet anise scent
and found two tiny triangular kernels
of seed missed by the birds,
crunched one between my teeth
and sucked the sharp-sweet licorice taste.
I gave you one and for a moment
I could see your mother's eyes, hear her say
with city-bred suspicion "Don't put that in your mouth."

I could see your eyes weigh mine
with a look as old as Adam;
you took the seed with bird-like grace
between your teeth and bit.

The Little Flowers

My neighborhood's newest dreamboat
taking his morning coffee. Flip-flops,
pajama top, hair screwy from bed—
girls in cupcake pigtails notice
the coy, coltish looks,
but off his meds the atmosphere
clogs up, he says, with goofy dust.
Joy or jaybird panic crushing
his skull, head cocked
at birds not flying past,
smiling up, heaven sunbathing,
loosing love to purplish ethers
in his head, now maypoling
the parking meter a million children
and me in shorts and Keds
round-dancing with him,
then back to mug and book,
tipsy rock-a-bye in his chair,
big head aswish, singing a little
Happy to be loved by you.
Dear stranger, keep it light,
Jim Dandy to the Rescue
or frivolous *fioretti* hymn
to your air of birds not there,
to irrelevant brick and sky,
to the Pacific so close still
not close enough to hear.

Sequoia

(For mi nieto, Ryan)

Tell me again why these trees are named Sequoia.
Tell me again what *sequoia* means. Tell me
how to prevent this boy's loss of innocence. No
tell me how to help him preserve his love of life
when it comes.

Sequoia sempervirens tower above me
as I drive this remote canyon to the New Millennium party. Hope
is what I pray not to die in him
though my friends will lecture me again
the loss is necessary for the boy to become a man,
that oldest heartbreak the world dies of. Sequoia

studied his daughter learning to talk
to understand language, created a written alphabet
that his Nation would survive. What
does this have to do with these trees, tallest, oldest
most massive that once spanned the Earth? What
does this have to do with hope? Boy and the man? What
happened to your girl, Sequoia? Your alphabet?

Old in Oklahoma you walked south
in search of the Old Ones
who left long before the Trail of Tears
knowing there was no hope, took refuge
that night in the Mexico cave, and
writing in your journal, died. Sequoia, I too

have struggled to write language, a poem
most won't read, maybe not even he, but a prayer
the roots know about not cutting down the soul. There is

no known natural death for redwood. No decay.
The oldest are still growing. Why
don't we study that? Sequoia

put me down to sleep with this boy forever, tell me how
to be the tongue of your girl, Ayoka, ancient
lullaby to his Kickapoo, the fog of all tongues
through the woods, this trail
of babel through the world's wordless beauty
to the boy he never loses. Sequoia

tell him how never to become the Man. Love
is why. Semper virens. Tell him
to study that.

(December 31, 2000, Cazadero)

Golden Gate

JULIA LEVINE

For the lonely, the bridge is a seam between two skies.
And sky, the lowest register of sleep.

Once a colleague of mine locked her baby in a room
and drove two hours out to this bridge to die.

And driving through these fields of mustard,
not even a glimpse of two bulls fighting in the hills

could keep my friend from climbing the guardrail,
skirt hiked up.

Now my daughter opens her mouth to the radio's song,
face turned toward the window,

and I see I was mistaken:
I've been speaking to my younger self all along,

swaying on the bridge up there, a handful of pills
sleek as bullets cupped against her lips.

Tell me, what is loneliness,
if not the strain of standing at the edge of all you know?

Look, my daughter says suddenly,
pointing to the ocean's watery nothing.

Hunter's Moon

Early December, dusk, and the sky
slips down the rungs of its blue ladder
into indigo. A late-quarter moon hangs
in the air above the ridge like a broken plate
and shines on us all, on the new deputy
almost asleep in his four-by-four,
lulled by the crackling song of the dispatcher,
on the bartender, slowly wiping a glass
and racking it, one eye checking the game.
It shines down on the fox's red and grey life,
as he stills, a shadow beside someone's gate,
listening to winter. Its pale gaze caresses
the lovers, curled together under a quilt,
dreaming alone, and shines on the scattered
ashes of terrible fires, on the owl's black flight,
on the whelks, on the murmuring kelp,
on the whale that washed up six weeks ago
at the base of the dunes, and it shines
on the backhoe that buried her.

Rain in January

When it started, I was glad
to see the sky cloud up with winter
the way it should. I unearthed
my boots, my overcoat, and went walking,
aiming for puddles like a child—
a kind of game I could play—
impermeable in the rain. Back home again,
I loved sloughing off my coat
like skin, then stepping out of rubber
with its faint damp scent.

Now I'm tired of trying to stay dry.
I close my eyes and remember
how you opened me as if I were all
doors and windows, your fingers and tongue
unlatching me to let the weather in.

At McClure's Beach, Point Reyes National Seashore, California

I would ask my family

Wait for a foggy afternoon, late May,
after a rainy winter so that all
the wildflowers are blooming on the headland.
Wait for honey of lupine. It will rise
around you, encircle you, from vast golden bushes
as you take the crooked trail
down from the parking lot. Descend
earth's cleft, sweet winding declivity
where California poppies lift up their
chalices, citrine and butterscotch,
and phlox blows in the wisps of fog, every
color of white and like the memory
of pain, and like first dawn, and lavender.
Where goldfinches, nubbins of sunlight,
flit through the canyon. Walk one by one
or in small clusters, carrying babies,
children holding your hands—with your eyes,
your oval skulls, your prodigious memories
or skills with the fingers. Your skirts or shirts
will flirt with the wind, and small brown rabbits
will run in and out, you'll see their ears first,
nested in grasses, then the bob
of fleeting hindquarters.
                    Now come to the sand,
the mussel shells, broken or open, iridescent,
color of crows' wings in flight
or purple martins, and the bullwhips
of sea kelp, some like frizzy-headed voodoo
poppets, some like long hollow brown or bleached
phalluses. The X X birdprints running
across the scalloped sand will leave a trail of stars,
look at the black oystercatcher, the scamp

with the long red beak, it's whizzing along
in its courtship dance. Look at the fog,
above you now on the headland, and know how much
I love the fog. Don't cry, my best beloveds,
it's time to scatter me back now. I've wanted this
all my life. Look at the cormorants,
the gulls, the elegant scythed whimbrel,
do you hear its *quiquiquiquiqui*
rising above the eternal Ujjayi breath,
the roar and silence and seethe and whisper,
the immeasurable insweep and release of ocean.

The Trip to Napa

You would have liked the drive.
I played Jimmy Buffett. You know,
"My head hurts, my feet stink,
and I don't love Jesus . . ."
I tried singing along, but ended up howling—
you wouldn't have known me.
I quieted down only at the stoplight
and didn't get lost, even coming home
when lefts became rights, and the scenery
changed like when we went counterclockwise
around the pond on Orcas Island.

The Culinary Institute was where
Christian Brothers used to be
and I wasn't ready for that,
but our tree-lined roads and
the Oakville Grocery were still there
and it was near ninety, like the day
we picnicked in the car behind the market
and I dropped the pickles on the seat
and when we went in for paper towels
you lost your keys and I had to pee quick
before I could look for them.

I was always the one who'd find things,
but since you died,
at daybreak, before my eyes open,
my body shifts to your side of the bed,
and every morning brings the same surprise.

November 26, 1992: Thanksgiving at the Sea Ranch, Contemplating Metempsychosis

You tried coming back as a spider.
I was too fast for you. As you
climbed my ankle, I swept you off, I ground you

to powder under my winter boot.
Shall I cherish the black widow,
I asked, because he is you?

You were cunning: you became
the young, the darkly masked
raccoon that haunts my deck.

Each night for weeks you tiptoed
toward the sliding doors, your paws
imploring, eyes aglow. *Let me in,*

Let me back in, you hissed,
swaying beside the tubbed fuchsia,
shadowing the fancy cabbage in its Aztec pot.

And you've been creatures of the air and sea,
the hawk that sees into my skull, the seal that barks
a few yards from the picnic on the shore.

Today you chose a different life, today
you're trying to stumble
through the tons of dirt that hold you down:

you're a little grove of mushrooms,
rising from the forest floor you loved.
Bob saw you in the windbreak—

November mushrooms, he said,
off-white and probably poisonous.
Shall I slice you for the feast?

If I eat you will I die back into your arms?
Shall I give thanks for God's wonders
because they all are you, and you are them?

The meadow's silent, its dead grasses
ignore each other and the evening walkers
who trample them. What will you be,

I wonder, when the night wind rises?
Come back as yourself, in your blue parka,
your plaid flannel shirt with the missing button.

These fields that hum and churn with life
are empty. There is nowhere
you are not, nowhere

you are not not.

Between

Fog and

Drizzle

Living on the Earthquake Fault

It zigzagged
Under my house, across the back of my garden
And into the hill. The tunnel to Solano Avenue
Cried tears out of the middle of the earth.
And I was the one who tried to hold it together. I grabbed like a clutching
                                                    grandmother,
Bridged the earth-slip with my spine.

When they said: let go, I said
I'm holding the world shut all by myself, soon
It will mend like a slit in an orange.

It takes time to learn the logic of chaos.
The open fissure
Ground up pebbles green as the coast of Ireland
Or streaked with blue like the bay, it spat out
Pieces of colored fire. My house sagged and squeaked. I went to look at
                                                    the view. It was
Extraordinary.

A vast new country, scarves of dark brown water,
It waited for me; it wanted my books and my children's mother;
It needed its name, and only I could say it.

Dog and Bear

The air this morning,
blowing between fog and drizzle,

is like a white dog in the snow
who scents a white bear in the snow
who is not there.

Deeper than seeing,
deeper than hearing,
they stand and glare, one at the other.

So many listen lost, in every weather.

The mind has mountains,
Hopkins wrote, against his sadness.

The dog held the bear at bay, that day.

Koi Pond, Oakland Museum

Our shadows bring them from the shadows:
a bright yellow one with a navy pattern
like a Japanese woodblock print of fish scales.
A fat 18-karat one splashed with gaudy purple
and a patch of gray. One with a gold head,
a body skim-milk-white, trailing ventral fins
like half-folded fans of lace.
A peach-colored, faintly disheveled one,
and one, compact, all indigo in faint green water.
They wear comical whiskers and gather beneath us
as we lean on the cement railing
in indecisive late-December light,
and because we do not feed them, they pass,
then they loop and circle back. Loop and circle. Loop.
"Look," you say, "beneath them." Beneath them,
like a subplot or a motive, is a school
of uniformly dark ones, smaller, unadorned,
perhaps another species, living in the shadow
of the gold, purple, yellow, indigo, and white,
seeking the mired roots and dusky grasses,
unliveried, the quieter beneath the quiet.

Landscape with Snakes

Eden Valley Ranch, 1956

Our quick-running silver was already
seeping, unseen, back into the slow ground,
closing commerce with the outside, the year
our mother sailed inland on a lotus,
limbs entwined, while her boys went on living
in the long dream of the fathers' fathers
where it was always summer, so it was
last August when we slipped from our cots
beneath the netting of the sleeping porch,
lying under Sanhedrin's shadow, and
swung our rifles up on our shoulders, our
flashlights bobbing in the dark, and parted
the fields of waist-high cheatgrass with our thighs
to the edge of the airstrip, where buzzing
like Cessnas above the world, we descended
on brush squats and nests of the cottontails.
Flashing our lights, we spun quick fire into
the soft white fur, and in the spread of blood
became entangled in the fescue grass
of fields our dreamy fathers named Eden.
Rattlers slithered over granite like streaks
of mottled grey from another world—
we took them for the water of a spring
until heads and tails rose up, framing them—
the wide, wedge-shaped mouths, the jointed
rattles dancing like rice paper, tsk-ka tsk,
ts-ka, as we circled now, fluttery as moths,
while in the summer palace of Sanhedrin,
our mother slept on, coiled in her bed,
and the cold-blooded, at home in Eden,
lay in wait for us, there, among the grasses.

WL 8338

I know a nameless lake in the Sierra
where lunker rainbow rise at every cast
and mating dragonflies
skitter above the surface
and hummingbirds with iridescent eyes.

No trail leads here. No ducks point the way.
Whatever route you find will be your own.
Nearby, it is so quiet
approaching through the trees
the wind is audible minutes away

and when it stills, the water's face relaxes
within its margin of untrodden meadow
and smoothes and clears to show
beneath what's imaged here
the undisturbed reflection of its form.

The Poet at Seventeen

My youth? I hear it mostly in the long, volleying
Echoes of billiards in the pool halls where
I spent it all, extravagantly, believing
My delicate touch on a cue would last for years.

Outside the vineyards vanished under rain,
And the trees held still or seemed to hold their breath
When the men I worked with, pruning orchards, sang
Their lost songs: *Amapola; La Paloma;*

Jalisco, No Te Rajes—the corny tunes
Their sons would just as soon forget, at recess,
Where they lounged apart in small groups of their own.
Still, even when they laughed, they laughed in Spanish.

I hated high school then, & on weekends drove
A tractor through the widowed fields. It was so boring
I memorized poems above the engine's monotone.
Sometimes whole days slipped past without my noticing,

And birds of all kinds flew in front of me then.
I learned to tell them apart by their empty squabblings,
The slightest change in plumage, or the inflection
Of a call. And why not admit it? I was happy

Then. I believed in no one. I had the kind
Of solitude the world usually allows
Only to kings & criminals who are extinct,
Who disdain this world, & who rot, corrupt & shallow

As fields I disced: I turned up the same gray
Earth for years. Still, the land made a glum raisin
Each autumn, & made that little hell of days—
The vines must have seemed like cages to the Mexicans

Who were paid seven cents a tray for the grapes
They picked. Inside the vines it was hot, & spiders
Strummed their emptiness. Black Widow, Daddy Longlegs.
The vine canes whipped our faces. None of us cared.

And the girls I tried to talk to after class
Sailed by, then each night lay enthroned in my bed,
With nothing on but the jewels of their embarrassment.
Eyes, lips, dreams. No one. The sky & the road.

A life like that? It seemed to go on forever—
Reading poems in school, then driving a stuttering tractor
Warm afternoons, then billiards on blue October
Nights. The thick stars. But mostly now I remember

The trees, wearing their mysterious yellow sullenness
Like party dresses. And parties I didn't attend.
And then the first ice hung like spider lattices
Or the embroideries of Great Aunt No One,

And then the first dark entering the trees—
And inside, the adults with their cocktails before dinner,
The way they always seemed afraid of something,
And sat so rigidly, although the land was theirs.

From Cole Street

a memory of Thom Gunn

At your front door all that week
new flowers, notes, a photo of you alone,
each morning I passed there I'd see
the tributes spread out to you across the stone.

You were gone. It was quick. That is all.
And now these remnants at your closed door,
words written back to you, prayers that fall
beneath that placard in your window: No War.

Even late, you wrote a book to love,
to faces seen through café windows, doors down,
to newlyweds, young neighbors you lived above,
to Cupid and his career, and your own.

Once, not too far back, you led me up your stairs
so I could question you (while my tape recorder spun),
about your latest book, those poems to the affairs
of other poets, of other loves, of lives done.

Nice biceps, you said through an admiring smile
as I pulled you into the past from your front room,
and prodded you about metrics, subjects, style,
and tried to take notes, and left too soon.

On the street I held my recorder to my ear
to replay the tape on which our voices crossed,
but only a dead hum, no trace of us left to hear,
my questions muted, your voice, lost.

At Moss Beach

At night along this coast the boats
slipped to shore with their illegal cargo.
The long cars waited, lights hushed,
for the liquor to be hauled up the cliff.
We've stopped at the edge of it this morning,
held by the lush purple spread of ice plant
in the hollows below. Whoever was here then
could not have imagined our lives, just as I
can't imagine the face of some new lover
after we're over. But the past opens so easily:
the stars sink, the prow cleaves dense fog,
the sleek unseen shapes of the limousines are humming
somewhere ahead, and behind the boat
the white froth of the wake travels
over the churning water. Packed in roped crates
are the bottles, in each one the rattle
of dice thrown down, a man loosened from
his money, a woman in a blue dress leaning
against him, the thrilling surf of her laughter.
Gliding through the dark, can the crew hear
our voices? You pull one vivid flower from its home
in the earth. I tell you it will always
make me think of you, this startling
brush stroke that repeats itself for miles
along the shore, this particular water
that today holds a freighter heading out,
a lone crow arrowing after it.

Oak Leaf

Holding an oak leaf over the campfire
in Muir Woods, I see its limits. A crude veil
of tendrils and veins stretches toward bright edges.

Along the surface a spider's misty circuit
crosses what already meets. Below, the shadows
of my fingers grow stout and narrow in turn.

I think they are my father's fingers:
a coarser nature, a worried popping of the joints.
Never still, his sculptor's tendency

to put every substance into form.
Wire sculptures he names *Spirit* and *Cosmic Fire*.
Each a chaotic relic of the path thought takes.

Its concave mending in lines never sure
of destination. A difficult mesh woven
into tunneling arms of copper and brass.

My art might amount to this: the meaning
inherited. My vision whittled from his, repeating
the same blind passage from stem to split light

in the captive shell. It's a Monday in August.
I can smell the ocean seven miles southwest.
My back itches from cold. My pant legs burn

against my knees. I'm thirsty and worry
I'm too late for something. I surrender
the woods, the red sticks flaking coals

in the fire, and the universe of the leaf
where black spots open to pinholes of orange light.

Bocce Ball: North Beach

Now they are bent
    on parenthetical legs,
        their vested bellies
round as the round
    of pasta in balls
        or cheeses in balls;
but, bent over bocce
    balls, clustered
        like sowbugs in circles,
they round out the roll
    of the slow-going, ever
        so slow-dying day.

What is the peace
    of this scene—the slow motion'd
        grace of their playing?

Puffing their bitter
    "Toscani," they play
        for a triumph in time,
for stakes so much greater
    than winning or bitter-
        sweet sips of Campari—
but pay for the mere
    statement of excellent
        gesture, the roll
of a fine conception
    down a long, uncertain
        course to a small, white
sphere, towards the pure
    joy of its light
        and an exquisite nearness.

Now they are rolling
    again in their slow
        unhurried grace:

when they do well,
    and the balls come
        daringly close
to the center of light,
    their eyes do not smile
        nor do they cheer
as young men might;
    but their bodies, it seems,
        on those scimitar legs,
with their arms bent
    like brackets—their bodies
        grow rounder for knowing.

Welcoming a Child in the Limantour Dunes

For Micah

Thinking of a child soon to be born, I hunch down among friendly sand grains ... The sand grains love a worried man—they love whatever lives without force, a young girl who looks out over her life, alone, with no map, no horse, a white dress on. The sand grains love whatever is not rushing blindly forward, the mole blinking at the door of his crumbly mole Vatican, and the salmon far out at sea that senses in its gills the Oregon waters crashing down. Something loves even this planet, abandoned here at the edge of the galaxy, and loves this child who floats inside the Pacific of the womb, near the walls, feeling the breakers roaring.

Bolinas Lagoon

Sink into a salt marsh. Walk out
and stand on black fragrant mud.

It will hold you, suck you down
with its slow viscous grip
until your rubber boots succumb.

Let your gaze go where it's deep,
past cordgrass and pickleweed,
where curlews press their runes
in newlaid silt, and bivalves
leave their bubbles in the ooze.

Watch the clouds cream up
in a cerulean sky, as the light
comes gliding in from the west
to land like a flock at your feet.

The ebb tide's last remaining
lamina of water makes the mud
a mirror where avocets walk
with ease, each bird tipping down
to touch its upcurved bill.

And you can't take another step,
transfixed in the sumptuous muck.

Land's End

As the light comes up, first shorebirds come in
one by one to tip the steepled granite
where surf breaks black to blue to white,
then their kin fill in quietly around and below
as a stream's bustle spills the tide sideways and slips
a bleached herring bone from its windowpane stone.
Plumes of gold bottle-grass never enlighten
the metropolis of igneous char and tilted slate,
nor do cormorants believe in the squall,
gravid kelp swales or sardines shivered down,
just as lizard and rock have different knowledge
of each other, yesterday, the gutted cliffs, the sun.
You may find you aren't needed, which is not the same
as unwelcome, and there is an order without design.

The Great Blue Heron

M.A.K., *September, 1880–September, 1955*

As I wandered on the beach
I saw the heron standing
Sunk in the tattered wings
He wore as a hunchback's coat.
Shadow without a shadow,
Hung on invisible wires
From the top of a canvas day,
What scissors cut him out?
Superimposed on a poster
Of summer by the strand
Of a long-decayed resort,
Poised in the dusty light
Some fifteen summers ago;
I wondered, an empty child,
"Heron, whose ghost are you?"

I stood on the beach alone,
In the sudden chill of the burned.
My thought raced up the path.
Pursuing it, I ran
To my mother in the house
And led her to the scene.
The spectral bird was gone.

But her quick eye saw him drifting
Over the highest pines
On vast, unmoving wings.
Could they be those ashen things,
So grounded, unwieldy, ragged,
A pair of broken arms
That were not made for flight?

In the middle of my loss
I realized she knew:
My mother knew what he was.

O great blue heron, now
That the summer house has burned
So many rockets ago,
So many smokes and fires
And beach-lights and water-glow
Reflecting pin-wheel and flare:
The old logs hauled away,
The pines and driftwood cleared
From that bare strip of shore
Where dozens of children play;
Now there is only you
Heavy upon my eye.
Why have you followed me here,
Heavy and far away?
You have stood there patiently
For fifteen summers and snows,
Denser than my repose,
Bleaker than any dream,
Waiting upon the day
When, like gray smoke, a vapor
Floating into the sky,
A handful of paper ashes,
My mother would drift away.

Last Breath

When the petals of the plum tree
swirl Up
before my headlights
I turn the car downhill and Drive.

Because I can't see
the way the apple flower
snows the air

the way the fever
of the plum
is brooding everywhere in Berkeley

I drive and I am driven.
Tightly smooth   and
forward in my black compartment.

Thinking things
that make me know   my
heart still beats.

Loving in a way
that will not get there.

So if I weep   behind this steering wheel

I say that it's ok
here in my privacy.

I can allow myself   one luxury.

Let it go now
as behind
the petals from the plum   turn brown
and blow
Down the dark driveway.

Sunset

Summer nights when I sit my front steps he walks his dog.
      He floats along on his toes, white haired and aquiline. Think
him an old hipster, musician maybe. Not cool, though. Nervous. Shy.
      The dog is a comma on a leash, so small and limp
it seems to say, "See, no bones in my pattering! I'm a
      cartoon beagle!" Me in my torn turtleneck, book and pen
across my thigh. I'm sailing the slow curve and burn of the year,
      staring down Haste Street into the sunset. But his dog
embarrasses me. His wife's? kids'? He treats it with patient
      avoidance. Sadness of man, sorriness of dog. Bobbing
storklike gait of his that wants to plunge ahead tethered to
      its tiny sniffing. Sniff, dispirited sniff sniff at
the roots of my unkempt hedges. Stops him, and he stands
      waiting, gazing off the other way. That dog is definitely
his burden, like the hats with earmuffs my mother used to buy me
      when I was a kid starting off to ghetto school. I didn't
bear those patiently. I simply lost them. He, though, he holds
      to the leash that punctuates his fate. Reminds me of
David, my old friend who lives in his famous father's
      shadow. Brilliant David, angled and darting, who hides
and grays there like a mushroom. Skinny, like this guy,
      hair turning white. Because of David I like this man
whose dog has sniffed us into sadsack connection we neither of
      us want. Stopped in the gap of my hedges on the pavement to my
front steps he's started staying, "Hi, how you doin'?" I don't
      offer much help, just raise my hand and smile.
I can see him over the hedgetop getting nervous as he trails
      up the block nights he senses me there. Dark
and sharpcut sitting sideways in my doorway. Like I'm
      judging him. In him I see my earmuffed white mommadom.
      Sailing preoccupied. But I raise my hand, don't switch off
my smile. Let nothing mean and sharkish gleam. He
      doesn't quaver, get peevish. We greet each other.
Friendly. Across the leash that binds us we make it alright.

The Bay

paddle around the little mouth
beside a large gap—   The Gate
the not-quite light chop yielding rusted nun buoy

lying farther out—   green wash unclear   no edge
nose numbing   toe vanishing
surface erasing surface of self   one becomes skin

or without skin   reaching nowhere
fog horn   quake-zone   absence is
eyes under surface   the living membrane   swim here

bone cold skin nip capillary constrict clipped off sting lips flip flop fat layers gone cold useful jelly fish numb-toed slop slung song overwashed and underworried the sea swishes its tail around drinks what it likes spits out takes in abrades harries the dry people rising sea levels melting polar glaciers beach front lot it's a matter of time lycra in the bay stretched belly rubber and polyfoam plastic goggles salt licking and licked can't help goes down the mouth tube how unsteady the land is when you stand up afterwards with ebb tide out the gate thousands of gallons in one narrow space the bay sinks 6 feet of water swept out solidity and substance flux flowing around itself buoyed up drunken

The Sun Is About to Pass

Friday 2:44 P.M.

The sun is about to pass
    from behind the last tree
    in the eucalyptus grove   Soon in a few
more minutes maybe five
            to spend gazing at the wild ruffle
    of scrofularia, coyote bush, coffee berry
          Just waiting, & waiting
       to finish and lie down
again while the sun keeps its downward path
         before drowning off Agate Beach reef.

Chin in hand I see them bobbing along the surf line
    in tender dalliance
Lovely to remember while the westward orb silhouettes
    the sickle shaped leaves of the grove
    and we'll soon be eyeball to light
    soothing the musing of expectation—
It's here   the moment begins.

November 17, 1989

Time Spirals

Under the second moon the
Salmon come, up Tomales
Bay, up Papermill Creek, up
The narrow gorge to their spawning
Beds in Devil's Gulch. Although
I expect them, I walk by the
Stream and hear them splashing and
Discover them each year with
A start. When they are frightened
They charge the shallows, their immense
Red and blue bodies thrashing
Out of the water over
The cobbles; undisturbed, they
Lie in the pools. The struggling
Males poise and dart and recoil.
The females lie quiet, pulsing
With birth. Soon all of them will
Be dead, their handsome bodies
Ragged and putrid, half the flesh
Battered away by their great
Lust. I sit for a long time
In the chilly sunlight by
The pool below my cabin
And think of my own life—so much
Wasted, so much lost, all the
Pain, all the deaths and dead ends,
So very little gained after
It all. Late in the night I
Come down for a drink. I hear
Them rushing at one another
In the dark. The surface of
The pool rocks. The half moon throbs

On the broken water. I
Touch the water. It is black,
Frosty. Frail blades of ice form
On the edges. In the cold
Night the stream flows away, out
Of the mountain, towards the bay,
Bound on its long recurrent
Cycle from the sky to the sea.

Contributors' Notes

KIM ADDONIZIO lives in Oakland and is the author of four poetry collections, including *Tell Me*, a National Book Award finalist. She has received fellowships from the NEA, a Guggenheim, and the John Ciardi Lifetime Achievement Award.

ELLERY AKERS is a writer and artist living in Northern California. Her works include a collection of poems, *Knocking on the Earth*, and a children's novel, *Sarah's Waterfall: A Healing Story About Sexual Abuse*. She has won six national awards for poetry, and her poems have appeared in *APR*, *Harvard*, and elsewhere.

YEHUDA AMICHAI (1924–2000) was born in Germany and emigrated to Palestine in 1936. A scholar of Hebrew literature and biblical texts, and the most important Israeli poet of his generation, he authored eleven volumes of poetry in Hebrew, two novels, and a book of short stories. He served as visiting professor at the University of California, Berkeley in the 1970s.

ELLEN BASS is the author of poetry collections including *The Human Line* and *Mules of Love*. She teaches in the low-residency MFA program at Pacific University and at workshops nationally and internationally.

B. A. BISHOP grew up in Oakland and Marin County, then attended Chicago State, where he was encouraged by Amiri Baraka to write poetry. He has taught with California Poets in the Schools and works with at-risk children in the Mission District of San Francisco.

STELLA BERATLIS lives in Modesto, California. Her poems have appeared in *Song of the San Joaquin*, *Penumbra*, *Rattlesnake Review*, and elsewhere. The title of this anthology is taken from her "Patterson Pass."

CHANA BLOCH is the author of four books of poems: *The Secrets of the Tribe*, *The Past Keeps Changing*, *Mrs. Dumpty*, and *Blood Honey*. She cotranslated the biblical *Song of Songs* and six books of contemporary Israeli poetry, including *The Selected Poetry* and *Open Closed Open* by Yehuda Amichai.

ROBERT BLY has published more than forty collections of poetry, edited many others, and has published translations of poetry and prose from such languages as Swedish, Norwegian, German, Spanish, Persian, and Urdu.

BARBARA SWIFT BRAUER, a writer, editor, and creative writing consultant, lives in San Geronimo, California. She is coauthor, with artist Jackie Kirk, of *Witness: The Artist's Vision in The Face of AIDS*.

THOMAS CENTOLELLA is the author of four books of poetry, most recently *Views from along the Middle Way*. A former Stegner Fellow, he lives in San Francisco and teaches at the College of Marin and the Institute on Aging in San Francisco.

NANCY CHERRY formerly published *Fish Dance Poetry Newsletter*. Her work has recently appeared in *Southern Carolina Review*, *Cimarron Review*, the *Dzanc Best of the Web 2008* anthology, *Cream City Review*, and others. She lives in Fairfield, California.

LAURA CHESTER has published many volumes of poetry, prose, and nonfiction, most recently *Holy Personal: Looking for Small Private Places of Worship*, and a selection of prose poems, *Sparks*.

MARILYN CHIN has been awarded an NEA grant, the Stegner Fellowship, the PEN Oakland/ Josephine Miles Literary Award, Pushcart Prizes, and a Fulbright Scholarship. She is the author of several books, most recently *The Phoenix Gone, the Terrace Empty,* a collection of poems. She is a professor of creative writing at San Diego State.

CATHARINE CLARK-SAYLES is a doctor practicing geriatrics in Marin County. Much of her book of poetry, *One Breath*, is drawn from medical training and practice.

DAN CLURMAN lives in Oakland. He is the author of a book of poetry, *Floating Upstream*; a book of cartoons, *You've Got to Draw the Line Somewhere*; and coeditor of *Conversations with Critical Thinkers*. He is a psychology professor at Golden Gate University.

GILLIAN CONOLEY is the author of seven books, most recently *The Plot Genie*. Winner of several Pushcart Prizes, the Jerome J. Shestack Award, and nominee for the Book Critics Circle Award, she teaches at Sonoma State University, where she is founder and editor of *Volt*.

CONSTANCE CRAWFORD graduated from the Creative Writing Program at Stanford in 1952 and lives in Santa Cruz, California.

PATRICK DALY works as an information architect. He is author of the chapbook *Playing with Fire*, which won the Abby Niebauer Memorial Prize in 1996.

WILLIAM DICKEY (1928–94) was chosen by W. H. Auden as a Yale Younger Poet for his *Of the Festivity*, and published fourteen other books of poetry. He was a professor of English and creative writing at San Francisco State University and chair of the Creative Writing Department.

W. S. DI PIERO's most recent book is *Chinese Apples: New and Selected Poems*. A recipient of grants from the Guggenheim and Ingram Merrill Foundations, he lives in San Francisco.

MARK DOTY has published eight books of poetry, most recently *Fire to Fire: New and Selected Poems*—winner of the National Book Award—and four books of nonfiction.

SHARON DOUBIAGO's *Love on the Streets, Selected and New Poems*, was published in 2008. Volume 1 of her memoir, *My Father's Love: Portrait of the Poet as a Young Girl*, was recently published.

ELLEN DUDLEY, author of *Slow Burn* and *The Geographic Cure*, is founding editor/publisher of *The Marlboro Review*. Her work has appeared in *Agni, Massachusetts Review, Phoebe, The Poetry Miscellany, TriQuarterly*, and *Verse Daily*.

ROBERT DUNCAN (1919–88), born in Oakland, California, was a leading poet of the San Francisco Renaissance during the late 1940s and fifties. His volumes of poetry include *The Opening of the Field, Roots and Branches*, and *Bending the Bow*.

CAMILLE T. DUNGY is editor of *Black Nature: Four Centuries of African American Nature Poetry*, and coeditor of *From the Fishouse: An Anthology of Poems that Sing, Rhyme, Resound, Syncopate, Alliterate, and Just Plain Sound Great*. Her most recent book is *Suck on the Marrow*.

QUINTON DUVAL has published three collections of poems: *Among Summer Pines, Joe's Rain*, and *Dinner Music*. He lives in West Sacramento.

DON EMBLEN (1918–2009), teacher, writer, critic, biographer, and botanist, served as Sonoma County's first poet laureate, 2000-2002. After retiring from teaching, he ran Clamshell Press until his death. He is the author of ten poetry books. A posthumous collected works is forthcoming in 2010.

DONNA EMERSON is a college instructor, licensed clinical social worker, and photographer. Her chapbook, *Body Rhymes,* was published in 2009. She lives in Petaluma, California.

MARTÍN ESPADA is the author of several books of poems, his most recent being *The Republic of Poetry.* The recipient of numerous awards, including two NEA fellowships, he has also edited two anthologies, written a book of essays, and released a CD of poetry.

PETER EVERWINE, a long-time Fresno resident, taught for many years at California State University. He is the author of four books of poetry, most recently *From the Meadow: Selected and New Poems.* He has also published several books of translations of Aztec poetry.

SHARON FAIN won the 2003 Pudding House Press Prize for her chapbook *Telling the Story Another Way.* She received the 2009 Robinson Jeffers Tor House Prize. Her work has appeared in *Poetry East, The Literary Review, Nimrod, Southern Poetry Review*, and other publications.

ANN FISHER-WIRTH published her third book of poems, *Carta Marina,* in 2009. She is the author of several other books and chapbooks. With Laura-Gray Street, she is currently coediting an anthology of ecological poetry. She teaches at the University of Mississippi.

MOLLY FISK is author of *Listening to Winter* and has received grants from the National Endowment for the Arts, the California Arts Council, and the Marin Arts Council. She lives in the Sierra foothills.

JEAN V. GIER is a writer and researcher in the field of Filipino American studies and has coedited two anthologies of hay(na)ku poetry. She has published her own poems in various journals and in the anthologies *Babaylan, Returning a Borrowed Tongue*, and *Going Home to a Landscape.*

SANDRA GILBERT's most recent poetry collection, her seventh, is *Belongings.* Her prose titles include *Wrongful Death.* A recipient of grants from the Guggenheim and Rockefeller Foundations, as well as the National Endowment for the Humanities, she divides her time between Berkeley and Paris.

DANA GIOIA, former director of the National Endowment for the Arts, has published three full-length collections of poems and eight chapbooks. He is also the author of the critical work *Can Poetry Matter?*

LINDA GREGG was raised in Marin County and is an alumna of San Francisco State University. She is the author of seven books of poetry, most recently *All of It Singing,* and the recipient of numerous national honors, including the Guggenheim Award and the Lannan Literary Award.

THOM GUNN (1929–2004), born in Gravesend, Kent, England, published more than a dozen books of poetry, from *Fighting Terms* (1954) to *The Man with Night Sweats* (1992) and *Boss Cupid* (2000). He died in San Francisco, his home of fifty years.

KEN HAAS was born and raised in New York City, went to college in the Boston area, and attended graduate school in England. He now lives and writes in San Francisco, where he works in biotechnology.

FORREST HAMER is a psychologist, psychoanalyst, and award-winning poet living in Oakland, California. He is the author of three books of poetry, most recently *Rift.*

ROBERT HASS has made his home in the San Francisco Bay Area all his life. The author or editor of nineteen books of poems, essays, and translations, he served as poet laureate of the United States from 1995 to 1997. His most recent book, *Time and Materials*, won the 2007 National Book Award.

ZBIGNIEW HERBERT (1924–98), an influential Polish poet, essayist, and playwright, is one of the most translated of Polish writers. His best-known work, *Mr. Cogito*, contains poems that were written when he taught in California in the early seventies.

LEE HERRICK is the author of *This Many Miles from Desire*. His poems have appeared in *ZYZZYVA, Bloomsbury Review*, and *Many Mountains Moving*. The founding editor of *In the Grove*, he was raised in California's East Bay and teaches at Fresno City College.

BRENDA HILLMAN's *Bright Existence* was a finalist for the Pulitzer Prize, and she has received awards from the Guggenheim Foundation, the NEA, and the Poetry Society of America. Her most recent book is *Practical Water*. She teaches in the MFA program of St. Mary's College, California.

JANE HIRSHFIELD is a critic, translator, teacher, and editor living in Mill Valley. Her sixth book of poems, *After,* was published in 2006. Her honors include the Academy Fellowship for Distinguished Poetic Achievement from the Academy of American Poets.

TUNG-HUI HU is the author of two books of poems, *The Book of Motion* (2003) and *Mine* (2007). He lives in San Francisco.

JOHN ISLES is the author of *Ark* and coeditor of the Baltics section of *New European Poets*. He received an award from the *Los Angeles Review* in 2004 and an NEA grant in 2005. He lives with his wife and son in Alameda, California.

ROBIN LESLIE JACOBSON has been widely published and has received grants and awards from the Marin Arts Council and Poets & Writers. She works with California Poets in the Schools. "Wildfire Season" was published in an earlier version in *The Steelhead Special*.

JOYCE JENKINS is the publisher of the Bay Area's poetry newspaper, *Poetry Flash*, and the author of *Portal*, a poetry chapbook. She has received an American Book Award and the PEN Oakland/Josephine Miles Lifetime Achievement Award.

ALICE JONES is the author of several books, including *The Knot, Isthmus, Extreme Directions*, and *Gorgeous Mourning*. Her awards include an NEA fellowship and the Robert Winner and Lyric Poetry Awards from the Poetry Society of America.

WILLIAM KEENER is a writer, environmental lawyer, and Bay Area native. His poems have appeared in *Water-Stone Review, Appalachia, Margie,* and *The Main Street Rag*. His chapbook, *Gold Leaf on Granite*, won the 2008 Anabiosis Press Contest.

CAROLYN KIZER is the author of two books of prose and nine books of poetry, one of which (*Yin*, 1984) was awarded the Pulitzer Prize. Her book of collected poems, *Cool, Calm & Collected: Poems 1960–2000,* was published in 2001. She lives in Sonoma, California.

AUGUST KLEINZHALER's most recent book, *Sleeping It Off in Rapid City*, was awarded the 2008 National Book Critics Circle Award. He lives in San Francisco.

JEFF KNORR grew up in the San Francisco Bay Area and resides in Northern California. He is the author of six books, including his most recent collection of poems, *The Third Body*. He is a professor of literature and creative writing at Sacramento City College.

SUSAN KOLODNY has published poems in many journals, including *The New England Review* and *River Styx*, and in several anthologies. She is a psychoanalyst practicing in Oakland, a teacher, and the author of *The Captive Muse: On Creativity and Its Inhibition*.

PHYLLIS KOESTENBAUM has published eight poetry books and chapbooks, most recently *Doris Day and Kitschy Melodies*. Her essay, "The Secret Climate the Year I Stopped Writing," published in *The Massachusetts Review*, was listed as a Notable Essay of 2007 in *Best American Essays 2008*.

JOANNE KYGER began writing and publishing in the late fifties during the latter part of the San Francisco Renaissance. She moved to the coast north of San Francisco in 1969, where she has since lived, writing, traveling, and teaching occasionally at the summer writing program of Naropa University.

MELODY LACINA is the author of *Private Hunger*, a book of poetry. She has published poems in many journals, including *The Southern Humanities Review*, *Poetry East*, and *North American Review*.

URSULA LE GUIN was born and grew up in Berkeley. She has published over one hundred short stories, twelve books for children, three collections of essays, and twenty novels. Her first publications, however, were poems. In 2006, she released *Incredible Good Fortune: New Poems*.

PRISCILLA LEE is a San Francisco poet whose collection *Wishbone* was published in 2000 as Volume 5 in the California Poetry Series. The book chronicles the life of an Asian American woman at the crossroad of two cultures.

JULIA LEVINE received her Ph.D. from the University of California at Berkeley, and lives and works in Davis. She is the author of three collections of poetry: *Practicing Heaven*, *Ask*, and *Ditch-tender*.

LARRY LEVIS (1947–96), raised on a grape farm in the San Joaquin town of Selma, was one of the finest poets of his generation. He wrote six books of poetry and received numerous awards. *Elegy*, his final book, was published posthumously, as was *The Selected Levis* and his collection of prose, *The Gazer Within*.

JEANNE LOHMANN and her family lived in a house near San Francisco's Golden Gate Park for more than thirty years. Her new and selected poems, *Shaking the Tree*, is due in 2010. She now lives in Olympia, Washington.

KAREN LLAGAS lives in San Francisco and works as a Tagalog interpreter and instructor and as a poet-teacher with California Poets in the Schools. Her poems have appeared in *Crab Orchard Review*, *{m}aganda magazine*, and the anthology *Field of Mirrors*.

MORTON MARCUS (1936–2009), the author of ten books of poetry, one novel, and several plays and libretti, taught for thirty years at Cabrillo College in Santa Cruz and served as a poet-in-residence at universities throughout the country. His *Striking Through the Masks: A Literary Memoir* appeared in 2008.

STEFANIE MARLIS has published three volumes of poetry: *Sheet of Glass, rife*, and *fine*. She is a recipient of an NEA grant and a California Prize.

JACK MARSHALL is the author of twelve collections of poetry, most recently *The Steel Veil*, and of the memoir *From Baghdad to Brooklyn*. His latest of many awards is a Guggenheim fellowship. He lives in the Bay Area.

JANE MEAD manages a ranch in the Napa Valley. She has written three books of poetry, most recently *The Usable Field*, which was published in 2008.

Tom McCarthy lives in San Francisco. His poems have appeared in numerous journals. He reports that he "can see the Pacific Ocean from [his] kitchen window, and spends a lot of time looking at it."

Stephanie Mendel has published in *Runes, Barnabe Mountain Review, Rattle, Poetry Flash,* and the anthology *The Poet's Companion*, among others. Her book *March, Before Spring* is in its third printing. She lives in Marin County.

Josephine Miles (1911–85), revered teacher and first woman tenured in English at U.C. Berkeley, was a major force in twentieth-century American poetry and the author of over twenty books of poetry and criticism, including *Saving the Bay*. The PEN Oakland/Josephine Miles Literary Award was established in her honor.

Czeslaw Milosz (1911–2004), poet, prose writer, essayist, and translator, was born in Lithuania and worked with the Polish Resistance movement during WWII. He accepted a professorship of Polish literature at the University of California, Berkeley, in 1960, and received the Nobel Prize in Literature in 1980.

Alejandro Murguía is a two-time winner of the American Book Award, most recently for *This War Called Love: Nine Stories*. His books include a memoir, *The Medicine of Memory: A Mexican Clan in California* and *Southern Front*, which won an American Book Award in 1992.

Charlotte Muse lives in Menlo Park, where she tutors children in reading and teaches private poetry workshops. Her books include *The Comfort Teacher*, *Trio*, and the recently published chapbook *A Story Also Grows*.

Jim Nawrocki lives in San Francisco. His poems and fiction have appeared in *Poetry*, *Kyoto Journal*, *Instant City*, *Collective Fallout*, and many other journals. His poetry collection, *House Fire*, is forthcoming.

Diana O'Hehir, professor emerita at Mills College, is the author of five books of poetry, two chapbooks, and five novels. Recent titles include *Spells for Not Dying Again*, *Love Stories*, and *Dark Aura*. Her awards include a Guggenheim and an Alice Fay Di Castagnola Award from the Poetry Society of America. She lives in San Francisco.

George Oppen (1908–84), a member of the Objectivist group of poets, published *Discrete Series*, a seminal work, in 1934, then gave up poetry for two decades. His *Of Being Numerous* was awarded a Pulitzer Prize in 1969. He lived in San Francisco for many years.

Daniel Polikoff has published two collections of poetry, *Dragon Ship* and *The Hands of Stars*. He is currently completing a book on Rilke and archetypal psychology, *In the Image of Orpheus: Rilke—A Soul History*.

D. A. Powell has published three collections of poetry, which have been called a trilogy about AIDS. He has received multiple awards, including the Lyric Poetry Award from the Poetry Society of America and an NEA grant. He teaches at the University of San Francisco.

Jim Powell is the author of *Substrate* and *It Was Fever That Made the World*, and the translator of *The Poetry of Sappho*. His awards include a CCLM Younger Poets Prize and a MacArthur Fellowship. He is a native and lifelong resident of Northern California.

Zara Raab is a fifth-generation Californian who grew up in Mendocino County and attended Mills College and the University of Michigan at Ann Arbor. She has worked as a writer and editor, and is the author of *The Book of Gretel*.

KENNETH REXROTH (1905–82), poet, translator, and critical essayist, was a leader of the San Francisco Renaissance. He is especially known for his translations of Japanese and Chinese women poets. His *Complete Poems* was published in 2003.

ADRIENNE RICH has written more than a dozen books of poetry and nonfiction, most recently *Telephone Ringing in the Labyrinth: Poems 2004–2006* and *A Human Eye: Essays on Art in Society, 1997–2008.* She lives in Santa Cruz, California.

KAY RYAN lives in Fairfax and teaches remedial English classes at the College of Marin. She has published eight volumes of poetry, most recently *The Jam Jar Lifeboat and Other Novelties.* Her many awards include the Ruth Lilly Poetry Prize and a Guggenheim fellowship, and she is currently serving her second term as U.S. poet laureate.

JOHN SAVANT is emeritus professor of the Dominican University in San Rafael and the author of *Brendan's Voyage and Other Poems.* His work has appeared in *The Southern Review, The Journal of Irish Literature, Commonweal,* and elsewhere.

ELIOT SCHAIN has had poems appear in *American Poetry Review* and *Ploughshares,* among other journals. He published a chapbook entitled *American Romance,* and his most recent book is *Westering Angels.* He lives in Berkeley and teaches in Martinez.

AARON SHURIN teaches in the M.F.A. program at the University of San Francisco. He is a recipient of fellowships from the National Endowment for the Arts and the California Arts Councils. *Involuntary Lyrics* is his most recent collection of poetry.

RICHARD SILBERG lives in Berkeley, where he is associate editor of *Poetry Flash* and a teacher of poetry workshops. His books include critical essays, translations of Korean poetry, and five collections of poetry. His *Deconstruction of the Blues* was published in 2006.

GARY SNYDER is the author of many books of poems and essays including, most recently, the fiftieth-anniversary edition of *Riprap and Cold Mountain Poems.* He has been awarded the Pulitzer Prize in poetry and the 2008 Ruth Lilly Poetry Prize.

GARY SOTO's *New and Selected Poems* was a National Book Award finalist in 1995. Soto has published eleven books of poems, most recently *A Simple Plan,* as well as three novels and many books for children. He divides his time between Fresno and Berkeley.

DAVID ST. JOHN is the author of nine collections of poetry, most recently *The Face: A Novella in Verse,* as well as a volume of essays, interviews, and reviews. He is also the coeditor, with Cole Swensen, of *American Hybrid: A Norton Anthology of New Poetry.*

AMBER FLORA THOMAS, a native of Mendocino, California, is the author of *Eye of Water,* winner of the Cave Canem Poetry Prize. She lives and teaches in Fairbanks, Alaska.

DANIEL TOBIN is chair of the Writing and Literature Department at Emerson College, Boston. A recipient of the Robert Frost Fellowship at Bread Loaf, Tobin has authored four books of poetry, including *Where the World Is Made* and *Second Things.*

MARK TURPIN lives and works in Berkeley. His poems have appeared in *The Paris Review, The Threepenny Review, Slate,* and elsewhere, and his first full-length collection, *Hammer,* won *Ploughshares'* Zacharis First Book Award in 2004.

LEW WELCH (1926–1971?), a member of the Beats, is the author of *Ring of Bone, How I Work as a Poet, How I Read Gertrude Stein,* and *I Remain: The Letters of Lew Welch and the Correspondence of His Friends.* It is assumed that he committed suicide in 1971.

WALT WHITMAN (1819–92), poet, essayist, grandfather of American poetry, and believer in the human spirit, was born on Long Island, lived in New Jersey, and never visited California, except in imagination. He revised and continued expanding his great epic, *Leaves of Grass*, until his death.

KATHLEEN WINTER has poems forthcoming in *The New Republic*, and has been published in *Field, Verse Daily, Tin House, The Cincinnati Review,* and other journals. Her chapbook *Invisible Pictures* was published in 2008. She lives in Tempe, Arizona, and Glen Ellen, California.

AL YOUNG, California's poet laureate from 2005 to 2008, grew up in rural Mississippi and now lives in Berkeley. He has published more than twenty-two award-winning novels, collections of poetry, essays, memoirs, and anthologies, most recently *The Sea, the Sky, and You, and I*, a CD of jazz and poetry with Dan Robbins.

C. DALE YOUNG practices medicine full-time, serves as poetry editor of the *New England Review,* and teaches in the Warren Wilson College MFA Program. The author of two collections of poetry and recipient of numerous awards, including a 2009 NEA fellowship, he lives in San Francisco.

GARY YOUNG has written several books of poetry, including *Hands, The Dream of a Moral Life, Days, Braver Deeds, Pleasure,* and *No Other Life,* which won the William Carlos Williams Award. He recently received the Shelley Memorial Award from the Poetry Society of America.

Permissions

David St. John, "Peach Fires," from *Prism*, copyright 2002 by David St. John. Reprinted with permission of Arctos Press.

Amber Flora Thomas, "Oak Leaf," from *Eye of Water*, copyright 2005 by Amber Flora Thomas. Reprinted with permission of University of Pittsburgh Press.

Mark Turpin, "The Aftermath," from *Hammer*, copyright 2003 by Mark Turpin. Reprinted with permission of Sarabande Books.

Al Young, "For Kenneth and Miriam Patchen," from *Heaven*, copyright 1992 by Al Young. Reprinted with permission of the author.

C. Dale Young, "The Philosopher in Golden Gate Park," from *The Second Person*, copyright 2007 by C. Dale Young. Reprinted with permission of Four Way Books. All rights reserved.

Author Index

Addonizio, Kim, *113*
Akers, Ellery, *74*
Amichai, Yehuda, *55*

Bass, Ellen, *87*
Beratlis, Stella, *23*
Bishop, B. A., *22*
Bloch, Chana, *44*
Bly, Robert, *117*
Brauer, Barbara Swift, *88*

Centolella, Thomas, *84*
Cherry, Nancy, *63*
Chester, Laura, *122*
Chin, Marilyn, *60*
Clark-Sayles, Catharine, *91*
Clurman, Dan, *73*
Conoley, Gillian, *48*
Crawford, Constance, *43*

Daly, Patrick, *25*
Dickey, William, *75*
Di Piero, W. S., *92*
Doty, Mark, *16*
Doubiago, Sharon, *93*
Dudley, Ellen, *46*
Duncan, Robert, *80*
Dungy, Camille, *8*
Duval, Quinton, *19*

Emblen, Don, *76*
Emerson, Donna, *70*
Espada, Martín, *39*
Everwine, Peter, *10*

Fain, Sharon, *71*
Fisher-Wirth, Ann, *98*
Fisk, Molly, *96*

Gier, Jean V., *35*
Gilbert, Sandra, *101*

Gioia, Dana, *82*
Gregg, Linda, *42*
Gunn, Thom, *40*

Haas, Ken, *119*
Hamer, Forrest, *14*
Hass, Robert, *65*
Herbert, Zbigniew, *29*
Herrick, Lee, *54*
Hillman, Brenda, *56*
Hirshfield, Jane, *106*
Hu, Tung-hui, *6*

Isles, John, *26*

Jacobson, Robin Leslie, *9*
Jenkins, Joyce, *89*
Jones, Alice, *124*

Keener, William, *118*
Kizer, Carolyn, *120*
Kleinzahler, August, *3*
Knorr, Jeff, *83*
Koestenbaum, Phyllis, *15*
Kolodny, Susan, *107*
Kyger, Joanne, *125*

Lacina, Melody, *97*
Le Guin, Ursula, *18*
Lee, Priscilla, *67*
Levine, Julia, *95*
Levis, Larry, *110*
Llagas, Karen, *90*
Lohmann, Jeanne, *45*

Marcus, Morton, *20*
Marlis, Stefanie, *31*
Marshall, Jack, *30*
McCarthy, Tom, *38*
Mead, Jane, *11*
Mendel, Stephanie, *100*

Miles, Josephine, *13*
Milosz, Czeslaw, *64*
Murguía, Alejandro, *37*
Muse, Charlotte, *24*

Nawrocki, Jim, *112*

O'Hehir, Diana, *105*
Oppen, George, *86*

Polikoff, Daniel, *62*
Powell, D. A., *32*
Powell, Jim, *109*

Raab, Zara, *108*
Rexroth, Kenneth, *126*
Rich, Adrienne, *5*
Ryan, Kay, *79*

Savant, John, *115*
Schain, Eliot, *69*
Shurin, Aaron, *52*
Silberg, Richard, *123*
Snyder, Gary, *51*
Soto, Gary, *7*
St. John, David, *12*

Thomas, Amber Flora, *114*
Tobin, Daniel, *36*
Turpin, Mark, *33*

Welch, Lew, *59*
Whitman, Walt, *53*
Winter, Kathleen, *72*

Young, Al, *68*
Young, C. Dale, *81*
Young, Gary, *47*

141

Sixteen Rivers Press is a shared-work, nonprofit poetry collective dedicated to providing an alternative publishing avenue for San Francisco Bay Area poets. Founded in 1999 by seven writers, the press is named for the sixteen rivers that flow into the San Francisco Bay.

SAN JOAQUIN • FRESNO • CHOWCHILLA • MERCED • TUOLUMNE •
STANISLAUS • CALAVERAS • BEAR • MOKELUMNE • COSUMNES •
AMERICAN • YUBA • FEATHER • SACRAMENTO • NAPA • PETALUMA

ABOUT THE AUTHOR

Mark Van Patten was raised by his predepression grandparents, who taught him to love nature, never waste time or money, and the value of hard work. Both of them were avid fly-fishers passing the love of the gentle sport to him.

Mark is a retired fisheries biologist, freelance author, and public speaker making his home in an Ozark hollow along the Current River in Shannon County, Missouri. His wife, Regina, three dogs, one cat, forty-five chickens, and other assorted farm animals fill his days when he isn't teaching fly-fishing and fly-tying. Living a homesteader existence deep in the heart of the Missouri Ozarks allows him to experience a true relationship with the natural world around him. Whether he is pursuing the elusive rainbow trout with a hand-tied fly or tending to his small rocky farm, he takes the time to wonder at a brown blossom promising a sweet treat from a pawpaw tree.